T0369395

I Know I Need to Change, But How?

A Guide to Taking Control of Your Life and Work

Janis Ericson, CHt.

IUNIVERSE, INC.
NEW YORK   BLOOMINGTON

I Know I Need to Change, But How?
A Guide to Taking Control of Your Life and Work

The views expressed in this work are solely those of the author and do not necessarily reflect the views of the publisher, and the publisher hereby disclaims any responsibility for them.

iUniverse books may be ordered through booksellers or by contacting:

iUniverse
1663 Liberty Drive
Bloomington, IN 47403
www.iuniverse.com
1-800-Authors (1-800-288-4677)

Because of the dynamic nature of the Internet, any Web addresses or links contained in this book may have changed since publication and may no longer be valid.

ISBN: 978-1-4502-1829-0 (sc)
ISBN: 978-1-4502-1830-6 (ebk)

Printed in the United States of America

iUniverse rev. date: 9/14/2010

FOR GAMMA

You taught me the importance of integrity, education, and service.
Your charisma and authority inspired us all to achieve our highest potential.

I'll never again forget to think BIGGER.

ACKNOWLEDGEMENTS

I would like to thank those that have influenced me over the years, particularly the following individuals.

My mom, Cheryl, for your unconditional love, unending support and consistent encouragement, without which this book would never have been written. Your dedication to health, wellness, and personal growth has given my life direction.

My dad, Bob, who taught me the value of having fun. Modeling your adventurous spirit has seen me through many challenges and awakened in me a courage I didn't know existed.

My sister, Jules, for giving me perspective and teaching me the truth about love and friendship.

My friend and editor, Joe, because your belief in me and my work gave me the confidence I needed to go further.

All of my teachers, from Richard Bandler to those in the public school system. Your knowledge, wisdom, and dedication to expanding consciousness and shaping lives is met with gratitude and respect.

My clients and students, for being my guinea pigs and my greatest teachers. Your trust and willingness to learn and grow, for me, is a constant source of joy.

And, most of all, to those that have challenged me and gifted my life with discomfort. Without you I would never have learned so much.

INTRODUCTION

The first time I got drunk, I didn't have a drop of alcohol. That's right. At age thirteen, a few girlfriends and I got together for a sleep over. One girl brought champagne she had stolen from her parents. As we had our fill, our heads got lighter and our voices louder. We danced, and laughed, and screamed. When an adult arrived, we thought we were busted. Until, that is, they pointed out the label – nonalcoholic sparkling apple cider.

What we believe is truth. What we see is what we expect to find. Reality is subjective.

When I first started studying Neuro-Linguistic Programming, I was constantly asked what that term meant. I began referring to neurology (neuro), explaining that human behavior, thought, and emotion is a direct result of communication between the mind, body and brain. I went further by asserting that language (linguistic) affects neurology, shaping our thinking and behaviors. And, I explained, the most interesting part is that the representations and strategies formed by language and emotion can be modified and used to change behavior and generate specific outcomes (programming).

But, while this explanation is true, it didn't often get the point across. No one really understood my definition until I started sharing my dreams. It's always been fascinating to me that I could share a dream with a group of ten people and get a different interpretation from every single person. Meaning, like reality, is subjective. And it became clear; both are based on, and filtered through, experience. Every time humans have an experience, there is the opportunity to develop learning.

Take, for example, the phenomenon of young Indian elephants tied to a post to keep them in place. When they're small, the elephants struggle, only to discover they can't break free. Interestingly, the elephants learn this so well that, even as full grown adults who could easily pull the post from the ground and liberate themselves, they don't even try. They "know" it can't be done. In this case, experience becomes a limitation on the elephant, one they never forget. But, some animals never lose their fighting spirit.

This is why I say, my reality is better.

One of my favorite songs by the Grateful Dead illuminates the importance of perspective. The lyrics to "Standing on the Moon," while intended to remain ambiguous, is a metaphor for the relationship between the band and the audience. The band experienced their shows from a unique perspective on the stage, which they equate to being on the moon, which most people think they would prefer. However, the band never got to experience being in the audience, enjoying the show.

Standing on the moon...but I would rather be with you...somewhere in San Francisco...on a back porch in July...just looking up to heaven at this crescent in the sky.

As both trainer and practitioner, I know what it's like to operate from just a single perspective. My experience as teacher/healer is profoundly different from that as student/client. But, I have been on both sides, and this variety of experience has been critical to my health, happiness, and success. Reality, after all, is subjective. If you don't have a variety of experiences from which to draw, how do you really know which reality you want?

It is with this in mind that I present this book. At times I share my experience of reality, and at other times I put forth options and let you choose. What you will find in these pages are stories, metaphors, theories and interactive processes that are flexible and allow you to shift your thinking in ways that work for you. I invite you to engage with the exercises I've included, as experience is what drives reality. Isn't it more exciting to actually drive a car than to read about driving? With this text you can experience NLP both as a practitioner and as a client, and you're bound to have an experience that improves your ability to help others, to sell your ideas and products, and to relate to people in a healthier way.

I remember a few years ago, I was helping my mother clear out my grandmother's house. I came across a note she had written to herself on her stationary. It was tacked to the wall above her desk. It read, "Think longer, think smarter, think BIGGER." She understood the importance of getting outside her limited view to consider something more than her current situation would allow. In the same way, the only prerequisite to this volume is the ability to use your imagination. Do you remember being a child, dreaming up creative uses for household objects, or pretending you were much bigger than you were then? The ability to imagine is within all of us. It is the part of us that dreams, both during the day and at night. It creates alternate realities and expands the limits of what we believe is possible.

Your imagination is run by your unconscious mind, the aspect of you that dreams, considers, feels, and believes. This is the part of the mind that Freud considered dark and scary, because his subjective experience of the unknown was dark and scary. I personally find it to be a beautiful place, full of possibilities and warmth. Tapping into this sea of creative potential can change your life in many powerful and exciting ways. Then, your conscious mind can begin to explain to you why to keep the good things coming. And this is the best reality I have yet to imagine.

How to Read this Book

I've had many students over the years tell me that they learned more in eight days of my NLP class than they did in three years of graduate school. While I'm flattered that they learned so much, I also know that incorporating so much material in such a short time can be challenging. The only way to create long-term learning is through practice. You won't be an NLP expert after reading this book. You will, however, have the knowledge you need to become one. To be truly effective in incorporating this material, do all of the exercises I've included – more than once. Do them at least two or three times, sometimes on yourself and sometimes on others.

Start by reading it through once. Then do the exercises. Then read the chapter again. Use your imagination to enhance your understanding. If you're serious about improving your life and work, you're sure to enjoy the journey presented here. Please, be serious in your pursuit of more fun!

CONTENTS

PART 1:
COMMUNICATION AT
WORK AND AT HOME

"When all other means of communication fail, try words."

INTRODUCTION:
THE IMPORTANCE OF
COMMUNICATION

Nothing is more important than quality communication. It's difficult to reach most goals without the ability to speak, write, or otherwise effectively communicate ideas and feelings. Instead you become more likely to be misunderstood, passed over for promotions, fired, dumped, or attacked. But good communication skills give an advantage in business and personal relationships and make it easier to get what you want. So, let's look at the basics of communication.

> **Communication skills are critical to the practice of NLP and to life.**
> When working with another individual, it is important to interpret verbal and nonverbal communication to understand them fully. In turn, sending precise communication signals makes you more likely to receive the desired outcome from the individual with whom you are communicating.

Communication is both verbal and nonverbal. Verbal communication is what we say, the words we choose. Of course this element is very important, as complete gibberish, such as, "Dog carpet the runs on," doesn't very effectively convey any useful information. The problem in this example is the sequence of words. Without the proper sequence there can be little understanding. But, sometimes, even though we say the wrong words people understand what we mean. This is because a large part of our communication is not the words we actually say.

It's helpful to divide nonverbal communication into two parts: voice tone and body language. Voice tone conveys information about the speaker's emotional state. Baby talk, the high-pitched gaga and goo-goo, conveys information almost entirely through voice tone; the words themselves are meaningless. In the same way people "speak" to their dogs and, if they use a pleasing tone, can say the harshest things and still make their tails wag. Yes, in most cases people understand words better than dogs, but it might be surprising how much we respond just to voice tone. If you've ever been forced to say you're sorry "like you mean it," you've experienced the importance of voice tone.

Body language works similarly. A person's body postures and movements convey their emotional state, but also provide information about their actual thoughts. For this reason, it's an even more powerful method of communication. It would be hard to believe someone flailing their arms is remaining "calm," or a person who's barely moving is very "excited." A lot of research has been done on body language, including facial expressions, how to tell if someone is attracted to you, and the signs of aggression. The TV show, The Mentalist, has popularized the notion that it's possible to spot a lie with body language.

So, to refresh, the three types of communication are verbal (words), voice tone, and body language. Which do you suppose conveys the most meaning? A famous study by Dr. Albert Mehrabian in 1967 found body language conveys 58%, almost two thirds, of the information transferred in most communications. The same study suggested voice tone provides 35% of the meaning of a communication. The actual words themselves: a mere 7%.

Communication Types

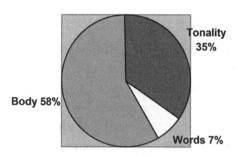

Most schools in the western world primarily teach the importance of word choice and overlook nonverbal channels. In light of what we know about communication, it's easy to see why there's such widespread misunderstanding. In this book you'll learn how to effectively incorporate these crucial nonverbal elements for greater success in all your communications.

CHAPTER 1:
PRINCIPLES OF COMMUNICATION

The following three principles provide an overview of how NLP approaches communication. Known as **presuppositions**, these concepts are the starting point for NLP and offer a unique way in which to understand and interpret communication.

Communication is redundant. Have you ever tried to not communicate? Assuming two people observing each other, it's impossible – even not communicating will communicate that you're trying to not communicate, or that you have nothing to say. This is probably obvious to you now that you understand the three types of communication.

Every word, tonality, and body position communicates something. The real issue is whether you're effectively getting across the message you want to communicate.

The mind and body are one. Are you curious why nonverbal communication is so powerful? It's simply because the body and mind are directly connected. In fact, they function so interactively and influence each other to such an extent that there really is no separation at all. Emotional information constantly seeks to flow from the inside to the outside and finds ways to do so.

The NLP term related to the mind/body connection is Behavioral Manifestation of an Internal Response, or BMIR. Despite the complicated language, this only means that internal experiences and outward behaviors occur simultaneously, that every thought and emotion manifests itself in external behavior. Therefore, one of the easiest ways to communicate what you really want to communicate is to make sure that what you're feeling and what you're "saying" are the same.

> **Try this at Home**
> If you're new to this idea, you may want to begin noticing how others react to your communications. One interesting exercise is to ask your friends and coworkers how they interpret you in certain situations. I had a client once that always got passed over for promotions. He couldn't understand why.
>
> So, I suggested he ask his supervisor for some feedback (using a curious and non-threatening tonality). The response was shocking for him. His supervisor cited my client's spacing out and obvious boredom in monthly meetings as his main complaints. Now, I had noticed that this particular client had a tendency to "zone out" whenever he was deep in thought, and we discovered that his body language was conveying the wrong message. Once he shifted his facial expressions and posture during the meetings he got the promotion he deserved.

The meaning of the communication is the response you get. An inevitable part of any interaction is that meaning is given to all aspects of the communication by the receiver. The message you intend to communicate is not necessarily what will be interpreted on the other end, though it does have an influence. Ultimately it's the meaning attached by the other person that determines the meaning of your communication. The response your communication elicits is the meaning of your communication, and is the result of what you send out.

This places the responsibility upon you to vary your communication until you get the response you intend to get. If I say to someone, "I love you," and the response is, "Aw, I love you too," my communication has been received in the way I intended. If I don't get that response, there has been a miscommunication. There are several reasons for this, which we will get into in later chapters.

If you want a different meaning or a different response, you must alter the communication. Being an effective communicator requires both the willingness and the ability to adjust your behavior.

CHAPTER 2:
HOW WE COMMUNICATE

One of the most important concepts for a student of NLP to grasp is what we call the **representational systems**. You learned in school that you have five senses, right?

1. Visual- sight
2. Auditory- hearing
3. Kinesthetic- feeling
4. Olfactory- smelling
5. Gustatory- tasting

Sensory systems are the key to how people understand, store, and share their experiences. These senses are how we take in information from the world. They help us to interact with our environment, and they keep us safe and alive. Your senses are what alert you to the location of a saber-toothed tiger about to pounce on you. They keep you from running into things and from consuming something that's bad for you (well, at least from anything instantly toxic).

The rep systems, as we call them in NLP, also assist us in communicating with one another. We are able to hear words, see body language, smell pheromones, and communicate through touch. Our senses give us vital information about who to trust, how our ideas are being received, and whether or not we're liked.

CREATING EFFECTIVE COMMUNICATION WITH REPRESENTATIONAL SYSTEMS

For one reason or another, we all have representational systems that tend to become preferred out of habit. Generally, one system tends to be dominant (or primary) for an individual – knowing a person's dominant representational system will give you a key to their pattern of understanding. For example, I had a client recently that used one phrase every time I told him something important. He would look up and say, "I see." In NLP, this is referred to a **visual predicate** (see sensory predicates below), and it alerted me to the fact that his dominant sensory system for understanding new concepts is visual.

Once you know an individual's dominant system, matching that system, by using visual words, cuts through unconscious barriers and creates more effective communication with them. In the case of my client, as he took in sensory information from the outside world, it was filtered through his primary system, which happened to be visual. When he sent information back out to me, it passed through the same system. Through his behavior and word choices, I was able to perceive the rep system he was using and take advantage of his natural inclination to create powerful and effective communication. When I used more visual words and showed him pictures and graphs, he was able to understand me fully and more easily.

As we will see, recognizing and pacing representational systems, is an important element in creating **rapport** and is helpful in conveying information to individuals and groups.

THE NLP MODEL OF COMMUNICATION

To understand how we take information into our neurology and how that affects our behavior, consider the NLP model of communication. Our five senses, sight, hearing, touch, taste and smell take in two million bits of information at any one moment. Our conscious mind however, is only able take in approximately 7 bits of information during this same time period.

In order to compensate for this vast difference (two million down to seven) the mind filters the events our senses take in by deleting, distorting and generalizing the information through language, memories, attitudes, values, beliefs, and decisions. We then make an internal representation of the world consisting of pictures, sounds and feelings that puts us in a state of mind, potentially changing our physiology and behavior. Of course, all this happens in a fraction of a second, and none of it has to happen in any particular order. But it also works in reverse: changing our behavior can change our mental state and our representations of the world.

This model is the basis of all NLP. We are in a constant state of flux, where our physiology can affect our attitudes just as easily as our behavior can affect our language. If we did not delete, distort and generalize the events we take in, consciously we would be in sensory overload. It's the sensation of more things happening than you can handle, which can be quite overwhelming, can't it?

THE META MODEL

The Meta Model assists you in communication by getting clear, precise, and accurate information. More accurately, the model reconnects a person's language to the experience that is represented by that language. This allows us to gather information that specifies a person's actual internal representation, giving us more information about the experience that created the presenting problem.

First published in Richard Bandler's 1975 book *Structure of Magic Volumes I & II*, the Meta Model features a set of specifying questions modeled on those developed intuitively by Fritz Perls and Virginia Satir in response to ambiguous and unclear language from their patients. Both were successful in their therapy by eliciting specific information about their patients' problems the therapists would not have otherwise known.

Clearly, the ability to gather accurate information is essential for clear communication. You need to know what is going on inside an individual in order to know how best to communicate to them. Everyone operates from their internal representations of past experience, what we in NLP refer to as a person's model of the world. People react to a given communication in the context of these experiences.

In subsequent chapters we will cover how to alter a person's model of the world, but for now let's focus on how to communicate within an existing model.

USING THE META MODEL

The Meta-Model is a model for retrieving deep structure from surface structure. What we say out loud is referred to as the "surface structure" of a much more complex set of perceptions and beliefs, called the "deep structure." In other words, surface structure is what we say, and deep structure is what we mean. The deep structure of language conveys many layers of information that is often needed in order to have clear communication with another person.

There are six main questions in the English language: who, what, where, when, how, and why. WHY is the only question that doesn't ask for specific detail. The answer to any WHY question usually begins with BECAUSE, followed by a historical account of some incident or incidents. This leads us away from accurate sensory representations. Therefore, we generally avoid using WHY during the Meta Model process.

The purpose of the Meta Model is to establish precise communication. It asks what, how, and who in response to the specific form of the speaker's language. For example, when a client says, "My dad beat me," you must ask "how" in order to understand fully what is meant. Dad could have hit them, or just won at a sport. If you decide that you understand what is meant by the word "beat" by simply calling on your own experience, then you are meeting the client in your model of the world, not their model.

GATHERING INFORMATION

Gathering Information is the simplest use of the Meta Model. With these questions, you'll be able to uncover and explore specific portions of the speaker's experience which are missing from the surface structure. **Deletion** is omitting data or selectively paying attention to certain of our experience and not others.

As practitioners, we must pay attention to our own communication with others. Errors can be made on our part as we gather information. Errors in information gathering can be divided into two types: Deletion is information left out as you represent the words communicated to you; Addition is information added by you, based on your own presuppositions or personal history, as you make representations of those words spoken to you.

To use this process, you'll first need to recognize when important information is deleted. You'll be able to identify this information by thinking like a detective. Pretend you're filling out a police report, and everything needs to be perfectly clear.

For example, if your teenage daughter says, "I'm going out," you're going to want more information. You'll want to know where, when, and with whom she is going out. You may also want to know how she's getting there and back, when she'll be home, and what she'll be doing.

Challenging deletions is critical in coaching and therapy. I've had countless clients come to me, saying they were depressed. If I only pay attention to the surface structure of that utterance, I will miss out on the deep structure. So, I often ask a variety of questions to elicit that deep structure, such as "How do you know you're depressed, about what are you depressed, and depressed compared to what, exactly." Here are a few more simple Gathering Information questions to use to recover missing information.

How, specifically?
Who, specifically?
What, specifically?
About whom?
About what?
Relative to what?
Compared to what?

For more complex deletions, such as **nominalizations**, you'll need to rephrase the noun as a process question. A nominalization is the deletion of a process, or the use of a noun when it should be a verb. For example, every time someone mentions to me that they're having trouble in their relationship (a noun) I see a ship in need of repair. I'm sure this isn't what the person means, of course. What they are trying to say is that they are having difficulty relating (a verb) with their partner. They are inadvertently deleting the process involved in their issue. So,

I respond with the question, "What's the issue with how you're relating to each other?"

One way to identify nominalizations is to imagine what the noun looks like. If you can't see it, hear it, or feel it, the word is actually a process verb. Some examples are hypnosis (the process of hypnotizing someone or being hypnotized), disability (the process of being disabled), and obsessive-compulsive disorder (the process of obsessing or being compelled).

EXPANDING LIMITS

The Meta Model also assists in Expanding Limits by defining and challenging the limitations of the speaker's assumptions, thereby generating more choices. This process is more therapeutic for the speaker than Gathering Information and can be very useful in coaching and management.

Generalization is the process by which components of a person's model of the world become detached from their original experience and come to represent the entire category of which the experience is merely a sample. In other words, one experience turns into a way of life.

The usefulness of a generalization must be evaluated with regard to the context. For example, the painful experience of getting cut from a sport's team can lead a person to generalize the experience into the belief, "I'm not athletic." The converse is also true. A person making a sport's team can create the belief that, "I'm good at sports." The value of the generalization in each case depends on the details of the situation.

There are several types of generalizations, each of which can be identified through the words they hinge upon. **Universal quantifiers** contain all, every, none, never, and always. **Modal operators** use words indicating a lack of choice, like must, need, have to, required, and should. **Presuppositions** are statements with multiple layers of meaning.

To expand the limits of a person's model of the world, there are a few options. You can call attention to a universal quantifier through exaggerated voice tonality, as in, "You NEVER win?" You can also ask for another experience that provides a direct contradiction to the rule. To challenge modal operator limits, ask, "What stops you?" and "What would happen if you did?" To challenge a presupposed limitation, add a presupposition of choice.

So, if I were to challenge the belief, "I'm not athletic," from the example above, I have several options. I could ask, "What would happen if you were?" Or, I could ask, "So, you can't even throw a ball?" Another option would be to ask, "Have you ever done anything physical successfully?" Below are a few questions that are useful in expanding limits.

> What stops you?
> What would happen if you did?
> Is that true?

CHANGING MEANINGS

The third and final use of the Meta Model is changing meanings. By reworking the meaning and significance of the speaker's relationship with himself, other people, and with the larger world, you are able to create lasting change. This application goes into even deeper therapeutic usefulness. By mastering these questions you'll be able to make significant progress with clients, friends, and family through communication.

While changing meanings can create positive outcomes, it is also responsible for many of life's challenges. Through **distortion** individuals shift or alter how they experience sensory data. Some distortion is pleasant, such as art or poetry, which often emphasizes sublime aspects of mundane things. Distortion in some sense is often necessary to plan for the future, to stay hopeful in trying times, and to make dreams come true. So distortion can offer choice in how we experience the world.

But distortion can also be very limiting. For example, a person that distorts a compliment with the interpretation, "They're just saying that to be polite," is limiting themselves and creating an un-resourceful model of the world.

Distortions are often stated as beliefs._To challenge limiting beliefs, you can ask, "For whom?" or, "How does X cause Y?" I had a client tell me she had to stay home because the world was too dangerous to go outside. I replied, "How does going outside cause you to be in danger?" Occasionally a person will attempt mind reading, as in, "John doesn't like me." To challenge mind reading, you might ask, "How, specifically do you know that John doesn't like you?" or "What leads you to believe that?" Here are a few more questions to challenge limiting meanings.

For whom, according to whom?

How does x cause y?

How is x equivalent to y?

Try this at Home

The best way to become comfortable using the Meta Model is listening to a friend or colleague's casual speech. Catch as many deletions as you can.

Once you've read the section on rapport in the next chapter, use the Meta Model questions to start asking for more information. Practice this for a week with as many people as you can. Then, repeat this exercise with generalizations, then distortions.

CHAPTER 3:
RAPPORT AND COMMUNICATION

When I attended my first hypnosis training, I was nineteen and easily the youngest person in the room by about two decades. We were directed to get into groups to do past life regressions, which was a little intimidating. But the instructor assured me all I had to do was make sure we had rapport. Then he sent me out to practice. It sounded like a great technique, this rapport, but I had no idea how to get it.

Rapport is actually a feeling of connection, of liking, of being on the same page. According to the field of psychology, you have to develop rapport over time. However, if you have the right techniques it doesn't take more than a few minutes to establish a deep and functional rapport between you and a client, friend, colleague, or anyone else.

- Remember, Meta Modeling questions beliefs that might be strongly held. To avoid defensiveness, it is necessary to have rapport – this can make the difference between effective practice and an insult! *Always use rapport in conjunction with Meta Model skills.*

- It is also useful to use a soft, compassionate tonality along with rapport to soften the experience of Meta Modeling, particularly when using command phrasing like, "Tell me specifically," or, "Show me what you mean." The process can also be softened with phrases such as, "I'm curious," "Would you tell me," "Can you give me an example," or "I'd really like to know."

Now, you understand that communication takes 3 forms: verbal, tonality, and body language. When building rapport you'll want to do so in all three of these areas. And, since body language has the most impact, we'll start there.

Building rapport is done through **mirroring** and **matching** cues like posture, breathing, gestures, facial expressions, tonality, word choices, and movements. Mirroring is done by creating a mirror image of a person's body language. For example, if I were to put up my right hand, and you put up your left, that would be mirroring. Mirroring works best for posture and gestures.

Matching, on the other hand, is done by creating a copy of a movement, tonality, breathing pattern, verbal predicate, facial expression, or posture. The most powerful form of matching is breathing. Now, I bet you can probably think of sometime in your life when you were breathing at exactly the same rate as somebody else. It wasn't an accident. You see this with smokers. They're all standing in a circle talking, one person lights up a cigarette and what does everybody else do? These are examples of naturally occurring rapport.

Let's look at how rapport affects intimate relationships. You might have experienced this one before: your partner comes home and she tells you she had the best day ever and is really excited. And you respond with something like this, "Yeah, I had a great day too cleaning up your mess, paying your bills, and fixing your car." This is, of course, accompanied by a gruff tone and arms akimbo. Rapport is broken almost immediately, and intimacy becomes a real long shot. In a relationship, both partners are responsible for building and maintaining rapport – you don't have to jump up and down with excitement in response, but you may just want to sound excited to hear the story.

But it's also possible to create rapport without the other party being aware. Rapport, for example, comes in handy at work. If you're planning on asking for a raise, giving a presentation, or managing a team, you may want to practice building rapport. This will create a more open environment for sharing and teamwork. When you have rapport, you have greater influence in a positive way.

USING BODY LANGUAGE TO ESTABLISH RAPPORT

So, now that you know what rapport is, let's look at how to create it with another person. The fastest way to generate rapport is to match breathing patterns. It's a little bit tricky, because some people are shallow breathers, but if you listen to someone speak its possible to pick up. You can also watch the rise and fall of the shoulders. Don't stare at a woman's chest, though, as you're likely to kill any chance of rapport almost immediately!

Other things to mirror and match are body posture and movements, but please note this should be done with subtlety. You don't have to copy them exactly, just lean in the same direction or cross your feet instead of your legs. If they gesture while talking, wait your turn to use a similar gesture. Otherwise you look a little insane, randomly flailing your arms. Only match when it's appropriate to do so. However, you can match facial expressions any time.

USING TONALITY TO ESTABLISH RAPPORT

Creating and maintaining rapport is essential for individuals that do business over the phone. If you make sales calls, book appointments on the phone, or make deals over long distances you'll want to practice matching the voice on the other end of the line.

Now, I should mention again that when building rapport you're not copying. You are merely referencing the communication in order to make the other person feel more comfortable with you. And, when it comes to the voice the biggest mistake most individuals make is in copying an accent. Please, don't do this!

What you do want to do is replicate the volume, inflection, and speed of the speaker's voice. So, if you're making cold calls, you'll want to listen to the person before launching into your script. Listen for the qualities in the voice, and match them as closely as possible. You'll be amazed at how well the conversation flows when rapport is present.

Using Words to Establish Rapport

Predicates

People choose their words unconsciously, most of the time, based on internal sensory representations. By paying attention to these **sensory predicates** a person is using, and matching the relevant sensory system you can gain greater rapport.

So, what are predicates? You've heard people say, "I *see* what you're talking about," or, "That's a *bright* idea." These statements let us know that the speaker is using the visual system. In order to build rapport with this person and ensure understanding, use other visual words in conversation. If the speaker says, "I've got a *firm grasp* on reality," you know they are accessing the kinesthetic system. And the phrase, "Life stinks," indicates the olfactory system.

I find this useful when giving presentations to groups. I remember being in college and having a hard time following this one professor. Looking back, he used almost all auditory predicates, which is not my preferred system. Yet, when an instructor uses visual words I am better able to understand. It follows then that by using a variety of predicates, a group speaker can address everyone. Here's an example:

"Now that you can all see my point is to promote environmental awareness, listen to all the reasons to conserve energy and resources. Then you'll really have a feel for how important it is to take responsibility and massive action now."

You may also run into a person that communicates using non-sensory predicates. I find this often with mathematicians and engineers. However, in those cases, stick with the relevant predicates. These will often put off people that use sensory predicates, so when working with a group you may have to choose between those two categories rather than including them both.

SENSORY AND NON-SENSORY PREDICATES

Visual	Auditory	Kinesthetic	Olfactory/Gustatory	Non-Sensory
perspective	quiet	touch	taste	think
picture	listen	smooth	stinks	know
look	noise	grasp	pungent	understand
vague	say	handle	scent	remember
focus	talk	firm	odor	consider
clear	tone	warm	whiff	believe
hazy	harmony	pressure	relish	learn
illuminate	sounds	tremble	essence	suppose
scan	orchestrate	stir	inhale	guess
vision	dissonance	penetrate	savor	ponder
bright	clicked	rough	fragrant	analyze
lighten up	resonates	cold	sweet	deduce
blank	loud	hard	delicious	put together
dark	rings a bell	fragmented	bitter	engineer
imagine	whispered	tapped into	breath of fresh air	
clarify	making music	weight lifted	sour grapes	
colorful	rumble	solid	smell it a mile away	

BACKTRACKING

Another way to build and maintain rapport with your words is to employ **backtracking**, which is nearly the polar opposite of active listening. With backtracking, you utilize the listener's words verbatim in order to put them at ease and speak within their model of the world. In active listening, you're encouraged to paraphrase a listener's words in your own model. This can be disruptive to the listener's unconscious mind, mostly due to the loss of meaning when words are exchanged.

To backtrack, just listen to the words another individual uses, and feed those words back to ensure understanding. For example, if I wanted to ask about a client's experience since our last session I may ask, "How have you been doing over the past week?" The client may respond with, "I did great, but I did go through a few rough patches." To backtrack, I would reply, "OK, so you did great, but there were a few rough patches. Let's work through those today." If I had responded by paraphrasing I would have said, "So you did OK, but you had a hard time with it." This would likely have been met with some resistance, because the words "rough" and "hard" are not necessarily equivalent.

PACING AND LEADING

Rapport building is of two types: pacing and leading. The pacing part we've already discussed as matching and mirroring. Now, let's discuss what leading is all about.

The point of rapport is to connect with somebody in a way that allows us not only to get into their model of the world, their mind, their reality, but to start shifting their reality into something more positive.

Let's consider an employee that's having a bad day. She's tired and feeling defeated after losing out on a promotion. But, you, being a manager skilled in NLP techniques, **pace** her by mirroring and matching her communication. After several minutes of this, you decide to lighten the mood by smiling and saying something positive. And, after a moment she smiles too. You've now successfully led her into a new state!

Leading is all about moving a person in a more positive and resourceful state of being. This is useful in just about every context imaginable. It improves teamwork within organization, personal relationships, and even interactions with service personnel. And the best part is that it's very simple. All that's required is building rapport, then changing your communication to fit the outcome you desire. There is even a formula for using rapport to effect change in another.

Pace, Pace, Pace → Lead

Sales people call this the "yes set." The individual stands in front of you with a clipboard, and they ask, "Do you love your children? Do you like to go on vacation? Do you want to have a better relationship with those around you? Then, sign this now." Pace, pace, pace, and lead.

The same principle works in a coaching context as well. Let's take the example of the client that is dragging their feet on a particular goal. Every time you bring it up they get cranky and defensive. If you're able to successfully pace their current communication and lead with a more positive and optimistic communication, you're likely to be able to change how they feel about making progress on their goal.

As the formula suggests, you'll want to pace at least three different pieces of communication. Choose from the posture, facial expressions, breathing rate, tonality, etc. Then hold this for a little while, deepening the rapport. When a few minutes have passed, you can change your posture or breathing rate and watch to see if the person moves with you.

Remember, you only want to mirror and match just enough that they start to follow you when you lead. You don't have to copy every movement the second it occurs. That's mocking! You're more likely to turn people off that way. All that's required is pacing one thing at a time, then switching to something else. You'll know you have rapport when the person follows your lead.

CHAPTER 4:
READING NONVERBAL CUES

UNDERSTANDING A MODEL OF THE WORLD

When it comes to communicating effectively, it's important to consider an individual's model of the world. What people experience in their lives, and how they process and give meaning to those experiences, determines how they communicate and how they interpret incoming communication. Therefore, if we want to communicate clearly with another person, it is important to know how they interpret their experiences (the deep structure). This will reduce the instances of miscommunication.

It sounds simple enough, but how can we reliably know what is going on inside a person when they often are not conscious of the process themselves?

We can never know all that goes on inside another person, but it is possible, using sensory acuity, to calibrate to the external cues of a person's physiology in such a way that we can know their internal emotional state at any moment in time.

CALIBRATING EMOTIONAL STATES

Language is a valuable representation of experience, but it is not the experience itself. Verbal language is only one way we convey our thoughts and feelings. We also communicate through body language and tonality. When you're communicating with another individual, listen to the words, but also pay attention to their body language. Behavior and physiology is a more accurate indicator of unconscious meaning. It is not enough to take someone on their word when they say, "I feel fine," or, "I understand." It is more useful to consider the way in which it is said than to rely solely on words.

Since every human being is operating from their own map of reality, filters get formed that habitually change the way we experience the outside world. It is important to remember to take this into account when interacting with others, because we must interpret another person's actions according to their map of reality, not our own. I'm sure you know what they say about assuming…

Calibration skills are about noticing physiological cues that indicate whether or not our message is being successfully delivered. This is different from interpretation, which some psychologists recommend. Not everyone that avoids eye contact is lying. Body language is often specific to the individual, and calibration provides information about an individual's emotional state and belief system.

The most important point about calibrating is that gathering accurate, observable information clues you into a person's map of reality, which works much better than guessing. Then, if you need to know more, you can just ask.

You may already be a skilled calibrator. Are you often able to tell when someone you know is upset, tired, or hungry? Or, have you been wrong several times or with people you don't know well? Either way, you will get even better after learning how to calibrate.

Calibration is simple. All you need to do is pay attention to a person's nonverbal communication, and then record it in memory for the next time it will come in handy. Here's an example.

A man comes home from work, and his wife is cooking dinner. She's got tears in her eyes, and when he asks her if anything is wrong she says, "No." Now, at this point you may be thinking that she's lying. But let's look deeper before making an assumption. Let's consider her body posture, tonality, facial expression, and breathing rate. When her husband walks in she's standing, bent over the counter, and she turns to him with a small smile. She's breathing normally, and makes quick eye contact. Now, do you know if anything is wrong? No! Not yet, anyway. We still need her husband to search his memory banks for the last time she looked and sounded that way. Let's pretend he does remember this same scenario from last night. And last night she had a tear with the same posture, and she mentioned chopping onions. Now, he can ask her if she just finished chopping onions. Success! Not only has he successfully calibrated her, he's probably developed deeper rapport for having taken the time to notice her.

Another way to think about calibration is the game *Two Truths and a Lie*. If you're a skilled calibrator, you'll easily spot the lie. The trick is, you have to pay attention to their communication when they're lying to be really effective.

> **Try this at Home**
> Find someone you don't know very well, and pay attention to their nonverbal communication during an emotional or stressful situation. Notice their posture, tonality, rate of speech, breathing, muscle tension, and gestures. Record this information on paper. Then, watch for those signs again, and ask for confirmation that the individual is experiencing that emotion. After a while you'll be able to do this quickly and easily with anyone you meet.

Calibration is also helpful when giving presentations to individuals and groups. Consider the instructor that never looks at his class but lectures from his notes. Is he likely to know if the class is even listening? Of course not, nor can he rely on asking his students. Some individuals may decide not to offend him or appear stupid, so they will deliberately lie. In this case, you'll need to know about calibrating incongruence.

CALIBRATING CONGRUENCE AND INCONGRUENCE

Here we will define **incongruence** in communication as a mismatch between communication types. If a person's words don't match their tonality, the communication is incongruent. Often this incongruence belies competing beliefs or feelings that are being expressed simultaneously. You've probably experienced someone saying, "I feel fine" yet they sounded and looked very un-fine. In this instance, they don't feel fine, but they don't consciously want to discuss it. In another example, if you've ever received a gift you weren't totally excited about, you may not have come across as believable when expressing your gratitude. What are the clues that indicate a person is incongruent?

I regularly ask my classes if they're following me on an idea or process, but I'm not listening to their verbal response. What I am doing is listening to their tonality, in order to determine their unconscious response. I know that if a student replies with a yes, and it sounds more like a question than an answer, I know there is a part of them that isn't fully in agreement. Maybe the student has 90% understanding, which is good. I prefer one hundred percent. So, I can use the incongruence between their words and tonality to determine the piece of information I need to rephrase or better explain.

More clues of incongruence are found in body language. Because, when it comes to congruence, verbal communication is unreliable. One way to see incongruence in the body is what we call **bi-lateral incongruence**, or a difference in the left and right side of the body. This can be the mouth moving to one side, the left and right hands doing different things, or leaning to one side. Imagine a line running from the top of the head down to the feet. If one side of the body looks different from the other side, there may be incongruence. One way to test it is to ask the person if they are unsure.

I find tonality to be the best indication of incongruence. Imagine the voice tone as a line on a page. If someone is totally congruent, the line is horizontal and straight. An incongruent statement would look more like a U- up, down, and back up. Got it? Was your answer straight or curved?

You've probably experienced this in your personal relationships. Maybe you've asked your partner if they want to go out to dinner with some friends. He may say yes, but his voice is a U. You'll know there is something he's thinking that doesn't fit perfectly with your plans. Maybe there is something he has to do first, or there is a certain friend he doesn't want to invite, or maybe he wants to choose the place. So, you can surprise him by replying, "What did you have in mind?" This will open the dialogue and prevent any miscommunication.

This may be a very simple example, but the same formula applies for other situations as well. So, begin listening and watching for congruence when asking questions. You'll be surprised by how much more open conversations can be when you're alerted to possible issues.

Summary

In this section you've learned the basics of communication, including the three types of communication; verbal, tonality, and body language. You remember that by mirroring and matching these pieces of an individual's communication you can develop a deep rapport. Once you have rapport you can lead the individual into more resourceful states of mind. You can also use calibration cues to draw inferences as to an individual's state. This is extremely helpful when trying to determine whether or not your message has been successfully delivered.

Here are a few points to remember when communicating with others.

- Always build rapport before getting into sensitive discussions
- Check on your level of rapport by pacing and leading
- Once rapport is built, feel free to lead the other person into the desired state to receive what you have to say
- Check in regularly to determine congruence on understanding
- Use Meta Model questions to ensure your own understanding and to help others understand you
- Meta Model yourself to be as clear as possible in your communication
- Be aware of your own incongruence, and express your concerns or stipulations

STUDY QUESTIONS

1. When is it appropriate to build rapport with someone?
2. What information is missing from this statement? "I just know you're upset with what I did."
3. Why is congruence important to clear communication?
4. How do you lead a person into a buying state of mind?
5. How would you respond if a client said, "I'm looking for help with my jealousy issues?"

PART 2:
EFFECTIVE INFORMATION GATHERING

"This whole creation is essential subjective, and the dream is the theater where the dreamer is at once: scene, actor, prompter, stage manager, author, audience, and critic." Carl G. Jung

INTRODUCTION:
THE VALUE OF INFORMATION
GATHERING

A man takes his car to a mechanic to fix the brakes. The mechanic assures the man the brakes will be fixed within the hour, so the man steps out to make a few phone calls. He returns an hour later to check on his car. The mechanic comes over and says to the man, "These brakes are better than new. I installed a brand new system that will outperform anything on the market. Take a look at how perfectly they work, and they'll never give out on you again." The man looks at the work the mechanic had done, and replies, "You certainly did an excellent job. That is quality work. But, that's not my car."

What people experience in their lives, and how they interpret those experiences, determines their future responses to other people and events. If you want to facilitate change in someone's behavior or emotional response, it's important to know how they're reaching their current response. Changing and fine tuning those strategies will result in their desired behavioral shifts.

But you can do the best work in the world coming up with solutions, yet if you're not specifying the problem, you're just spinning your wheels. This section is all about gathering information from others, like clients, coworkers, even yourself in order to determine what needs to be changed, and where. If you don't take the time to ask the right questions, you'll be solving the wrong problem.

Imagine this: a person calls you on the phone and asks if you're able to help them. What's your first thought? Well, if you learned anything from the previous module, you know to use the Meta Model question, "Help with what, specifically?" They may answer that they want to stop smoking, which is helpful information, but it's still not necessarily enough to make the change. In order to make a useful and permanent change, or even to communicate clearly with another individual, it helps to have more information and to know which questions will elicit that information.

It sounds simple enough, but how can we reliably know what is going on inside a person when they themselves often are not conscious of their mental processes? We'll never know everything that goes on inside another person, but NLP identifies some key pieces to the puzzle, and we have techniques for gathering reliable information regarding a person's internal process.

For example, one of these techniques is observing accessing cues, which makes it possible to know if a person is making pictures, talking to themselves, listening to internal tapes, feeling an emotion, or some combination or sequence of the above. Learning how to reliably gather this information is the foundation for eliciting specific behavioral strategies.

This section is geared towards finding the necessary information you need in order to make an emotional or behavioral shift in yourself and in your clients. Whether you're a coach, a manager, or simply someone looking for personal benefit the following chapters will give you the necessary tools to troubleshoot personal and team effectiveness.

CHAPTER 5:
SETTING POSITIVE OUTCOMES

The number one reason people and businesses fail is that they fail to set well formed outcomes. Instead, they may set a goal or just hope to succeed. These are not good strategies for getting where you want to be. Consider the example of the prospective traveler that calls his local travel agent. He expresses a desire to go on vacation, but only says he doesn't want to end up in Missouri. How likely is it that the agent will book him on a flight to Hawaii?

NLP modelers have discovered some very important elements to setting achievable outcomes, termed **Well-Formed Outcomes**. These are different than goals in that goals are more like dreams. If you've watched American Idol even once you've seen plenty of auditions by talent-less individuals with the goal of being a famous singer. But goals aren't necessarily realistic or achievable. Outcomes, on the other hand, are both realistic and achievable, and they include a strategy for achieving results. Whether you're an individual seeking to achieve a specific goal or an organization creating a business plan, you'll want to pay close attention to the following information.

An outcome provides a focus for what you want to achieve, the expected effects, and the resources required to achieve it. It is beneficial to set an outcome for all your goals. If you have not set an outcome for an afternoon with a friend who has herself set a specific outcome for your time together, then your friend is more likely to get what she wants.

You can get angry at being taken advantage of, but you were complicit in the outcome all along.

If you're not happy with how things are going in your life and work, there is a good probability you're not setting well formed outcomes. Symptoms of poorly defined outcomes are limited accomplishment, overworking, and becoming overwhelmed. On the other hand, well defined outcomes assist you in making helpful decisions and assessing your progress.

Well Formed Outcomes meet six criteria: 1) they focus on what you want, not what you don't want, 2) the outcome is self initiated and maintained, 3) the outcome is framed in a specific context, 4) the outcome maintains the positive value of the current behavior, 5) the outcome is worth what it will take to achieve it, 6) it is represented in pictures, sounds, and feelings. Let's look further into these six criteria.

1. Focus on what you want, rather than on what you don't want. A Well Formed Outcome must be stated in the positive. By stating what you want, rather than what you don't want, you set your focus toward what you want to achieve. I've had several clients come to me for weight loss, and when I ask them their strategy for dieting I often get the same response, "I tell myself not to eat junk food anymore." Now, when you put your energy into NOT eating junk food, there is little brain space for eating healthy food. So, when setting outcomes be sure to focus on what you do want. You'll have your whole brain and mind working with you.

2. Make sure the outcome is in self-initiated and maintained pieces. The outcome should also be something that is within your own control. For example, I had a client that called me and asked me to work with her so she could get a job as a TV host. I explained that I could help her give the best interview possible, but that I couldn't ensure that she would be hired. The reason for this is that I had no control over whether or not they hired her, but I could increase her chances with NLP. Again, by meeting this condition you ensure your energy and effort is well placed.

3. Frame the outcome within a specific context. When setting an outcome, you may also want to give it some parameters. For instance, where would you like it to happen? When do you intend to be complete? And, with whom do you want to work? Maybe not all of these questions are relevant to your outcome, but they are worth asking. Certainly giving your outcome a time frame is important. I can imagine many well known artists once said, "I'll be famous one day." And they probably did, post mortem. So, be clear. When do you want to start, and do you need or want help?

4. *Be sure to maintain the positive value in not achieving the outcome.* What needs are being satisfied by you not getting moving on your goals? Are you rearranging the sock drawer instead of filing your taxes or binging on potato chips instead of going to the gym? If so, look at what emotional needs those behaviors are satisfying. Then, find another way to satisfy those needs while still moving towards your goal. We will explore this further in Chapter 11.

5. *Check to make sure the outcome is worth what it will take to achieve it.* A person who pursues his outcome without regard for the impact on other systems (e.g., body systems, family, work environment, community), has not taken into account the *ecology* frame. For example, going on the Atkins diet may result in a good-looking body, but is the diet good for your immune system? For an outcome that you have at work, what is the effect on your family responsibilities, and can you mitigate any negative effects?

This ecology frame is of utmost importance to being successful and to enjoying success. No one wants to make progress in one area only to lose out in another, but this is all too common.

6. *Represent the outcome in sensory information.* This frame considers how you will know when you have achieved your outcome. What will be the sensory experience letting you know you're done?

I often remind my students of a funny example of this concept. I was in Belize many years ago working with two other NLP trainers. We were sitting in hammocks during a class break, sipping virgin daiquiris and talking about life. The sun was shining, and the beach was devoid of human inhabitance. We were there alone with the birds. And one trainer mentions that he wishes he had more free time. The other agrees that our schedule is too full. We have to be training 10 hours a days for 14 days in a row. There's just no free time to truly enjoy life.

These two individuals went on like this for some time, until I stood up and looked directly at them and said, "It's a Monday at 2pm. We're sitting on the beach in Belize on an all-expenses paid trip! You've got to be kidding when you say you have no free time!" Clearly these people didn't have the same sensory evidence of free time as I did!

The evidence frame is also used as a gauge to assess how well you are progressing towards your outcome, which helps you to know if any adjustments need to be made or if the outcome should be modified.

Well-Formed Outcome Worksheet

1. What I want: _____

_____

2. Does the success of my goal depend on anyone else? _____

_____

3. Where, when, and with whom do I want it? _____

_____

4. What are the benefits in not achieving the goal? _____

_____

5. Is it worth what it will take to achieve it? _____

_____

6. What will I see, hear, and feel when I'm successful? _____

_____

Now, let's put it all together. Make any changes to the original goal and write it below.

Well Formed Outcome: _____

_____

_____

_____

_____

____ Is the outcome achievable?
____ Is success measurable? Will you know when you've achieved it?

AS IF FRAME

This frame is based on the work of Milton Erickson and is based on acting "as if" a desired state or outcome has been achieved. When negotiating or problem solving in business and personal relationships, you can explore resolutions by saying, "Let's proceed as if I agree. What would be the next step, and what concessions would you be willing to make?"

If a key person is missing in a discussion, you may say, "Let's pretend Mom is here. What would she suggest right now?" Acting as if you have already achieved your outcome provides a very different perspective. It bypasses limitations of time and gives you experience of your desired future. It can also be utilized to gather information from your future self that you might not have had access to in the present state.

For project planning, you might want to act as if the project has been successfully completed and then ask what steps were necessary to reach this outcome. This approach can highlight some important parts of the process that might not be obvious when planning from the present forward.

When you place yourself in second position, looking out from within an expert's mind and body, you are given a completely different perspective and volume of information. This process, called **modeling**, will be explained in greater detail towards the end of this book. The **"as if" frame** is used quite often in NLP modeling.

CHAPTER 6:
GATHERING UNCONSCIOUS
INFORMATION

Now that you know how to set positive outcomes and get moving toward them, it's time to discover how to identify obstacles to success. Have you ever caught yourself making a new year's resolution only to lose motivation in a few weeks? Or maybe you told everyone about a great idea you had, but then you never did anything to make it happen. These are good examples of when the best intentions go unfulfilled, and I'm about to show you how to uncover barriers in your path before you stumble into them.

EYE ACCESSING

Have you ever heard the expression "the eyes are the windows to the soul?" You probably didn't realize just how true it is! Most people spend their whole lives never knowing what you can learn from the eyes.

Accessing cues are one of the most fascinating and useful pieces of information I have ever learned. With it you can literally discover what another individual is thinking, or at least which representational system is being used and whether it is a memory or the imagination at work.

Every person has a way of storing sensory information. There is an internal filing system that keeps information organized in the mind. Things we see get stored in the visual system file, sounds get stored in the auditory file, and so on. By paying attention to an individual's eye movements, you can determine the file in which this information is stored.

Now, there is a "standard" way of organizing sensory information. **Visual** (V) information is always stored at eye level and above, **auditory** (A) information at ear level, **kinesthetic** (K) information is stored down to the individual's right, and self talk, or **auditory internal** (Ai), is always down to a person's left.

But, just as you have your own way of filing documents, there may also be slight differences between individuals in regards to the location of specific visual and auditory information. There are two types of visual (V) and auditory (A) information- remembered (r) and constructed (c). Remembered information is something that has been experienced in the real world (like seeing a sea lion swimming). Constructed information is generated by the imagination (imagining the sea lion in another setting). If you reference the eye accessing chart above, you'll notice that constructed information is on the left, while remember information is on the right. However, this is not always the case. Some people have constructed information on the right. And, to make it even more interesting, some people store visual constructed information and auditory constructed information on different sides! The only way you will know a person's filing system for sure is to ask some sensory based questions, or by listening to emotionally sensitive information. Try asking the questions below in order to map someone's filing system.

EYE ACCESSING QUESTIONS

Visual Remembered:	What does _____ look like?
	What is the color of _____?
Visual Constructed:	Can you imagine the view from Machu Pichu?
	What would a cat look like with an elephant's body?
	Could you imagine a _____ becoming a _____?
Auditory Remembered:	What's the sound of _____?
	What does your favorite song sound like?
Auditory Constructed:	What does _____ changing into_____ sound like?
	What does your favorite song sound like sung by chipmunks?
	What does a whistle sound like under water?
Auditory Digital:	What is something you say to yourself to get yourself out of bed?
	What does your own voice sound like in your head?
Kinesthetic:	What did it feel like the first time you fell in love?
	How does the sun feel when it's on your back?
	How did you feel when you got your first paycheck?
Olfactory/Gustatory:	What does a lemon taste like when you bite into it?
	How does fresh cut grass smell?
	How does chocolate taste after a sip of red wine?

BODY ACCESSING

There are some cultures on planet Earth that find it rude to move the eyes or to look someone in the eye. When working with these individuals you are unlikely to be able to use eye accessing. But you're in luck! Many people prefer to access information using body movements, and some individuals will do both simultaneously.

Body accessing works in the same way as eye accessing; the quadrants are organized in the same way. The only difference is that you're focusing on the whole body at once. A trick to make this easier is to stand back and view the individual in your peripheral, or expanded, vision. This makes it easier to catch everything. I once had a student that I was working with in front of the class. I kept waiting for a kinesthetic eye access, but what I didn't realize was that his right foot was bouncing like crazy! I was just so focused on his eyes that I missed out on the true access.

Body accessing includes:

- Moving the mouth
- Foot or hand tapping
- Head nodding (side to side, usually)
- Leaning (with the head or shoulders)
- Lateral crossing (arms or legs)

THE VALUE OF ACCESSING

Now, you may be wondering what to do with this information, so let me satisfy your curiosity. Once you have discovered what sensory system is being accessed, and whether it is a memory or the imagination being used, you'll want to reveal the actual representation. For example, I had a client years ago that was dealing with severe jealousy. She was constantly suspicious of every man she dated. And when I asked her how she knew he was being unfaithful, she accessed a Visual Constructed image. This indicated to me that she was just imagining it happening! So, I asked her if she had ever caught a man cheating on her. I wasn't surprised when she said no.

Having this information was tremendously helpful in working with her. I had enough information to know I wasn't dealing with a traumatic memory, but a tendency to create problems where none exist. The approach for these two possibilities is drastically different.

Now, I also had to find out what the picture was she was creating in her mind's eye. So I asked, "When you get jealous, what are you imagining happening?" Note that I used visual constructed language because that was the quadrant she was accessing. She replied, "I see him leaving me and finding someone else that's prettier and smarter." With this information I knew she was making a movie to cause her jealousy. This information gave me what I needed to begin helping her make a change. In subsequent chapters I will explain to do that as well.

Try this at Home

The next time you sit down with a friend or colleague, ask them about their weekend. Pay attention to the words they use and how the words correspond to their eye and body accessing. Some times they match, and other times they don't.

Once you've developed the habit of checking for accessing cues, begin asking specific questions to uncover the representations being accessed. Here are a few sample questions to get you started. Remember to pay attention to both eye and body accessing cues.

What did that look like?
How did that sound?
How did that make you feel?
How do you imagine that happening?
What do you imagine that sounding like?
When you imagine that happening, how do you feel?

CHAPTER 7:
THE MAP IS NOT THE TERRITORY.

"A map is not the territory it represents, but if correct, it has a similar structure to the territory, which accounts for its usefulness." A. Korzybski, Science and Sanity

Consider this for a moment: there is a distinct difference between the "real" world and your interpretation of it. This interpretation becomes your map, which you use as a frame of reference for your current behavior. For example, you can put ten people in the same room with a teacher. If the teacher warns the class there will be a pop quiz, you'll have a variety of responses. There are the Lisa Simpsons of the world who are thrilled at the chance to prove their intelligence. There are also the Barts, who couldn't care less. You might also have those that panic because they doubt their own abilities, or possibly the teacher's abilities.

So, your representations of the world determine what your experience and response to the world will be. You respond to your map of reality, not to reality itself. But this is a powerfully liberating realization, because it means that in order to change your response, you don't have to change reality. You can simply change your map.

WHAT MAKES UP OUR REALITY?

Human beings are like snowflakes, no two experience the world in the exact same way. You are unique, and you create a representation of reality to guide you in the world. This model of the world, or reality strategy, is based upon both your programming and the meaning you gave to your personal experiences.

There are five basic elements that create your map, or model of the world that take place within a given context or situation.

Pretend for a moment that you're sitting at the beach. Consider how you feel, what you imagine doing, why you're there, and what you're getting out of being at the beach. Now contrast that experience with going in to work. Again, consider how you feel, what you imagine doing, why you're there, and what you're getting out of going to work.

The content of the two experiences are often different, unless you either love your job or hate the beach! In all seriousness though, you probably feel and respond differently in different contexts. And how you respond is different from how I respond, and so on.

So, what are the relevant elements of information that you want to gather in order to begin coaching yourself or someone else towards a positive behavioral shift?

- The internal state, an emotional or mental state of being, feelings
- The actual behaviors and/or personal physiology
- The internal computations, or mental strategies and internal thoughts
- The criteria, or values, that are driving the behaviors
- And the relevant beliefs being held by the individual

These elements are explained in greater detail below.

PRESENT V. DESIRED STATES

In NLP, the **present state** is a description of the mental and emotional state of an individual or group in regards to an outcome that they have selected. The **desired state** is simply the preferred state for optimal performance. These states have a structure to them; they are made up of the five elements listed above.

By gathering the structure of these states, you're able to identify where the major obstacles to success lie. As an example, one of the first clients I had when I began my practice could not understand why no one was able to help her get ahead in life. After some serious rapport- building and Meta

Modeling, I discovered she felt angry most of the time. Her physiology supported that emotional state, as she usually had her chest thrust forward and her eyes were often squinted. This was her present state.

I also found out that she spent a great deal of her time blaming her previous partners for ruining her life. When I asked her what positive intention this blaming behavior was providing, she was able to admit that it kept her out of despair. And she truly believed that the only way to make it in the world was through lying and cheating other people. Of course, after I heard this, I made her pay for her sessions up front!

And, as you may have guessed, this structure was not helping her become a top seller. For that matter, it kept her unemployed. And having had the opportunity to model several successful salespeople, I had a clue as to how to structure her desired state. And, armed with this information, I was able to begin doing change work with her. I'll discuss this in more detail in subsequent chapters.

Business consultants use NLP to observe an organization and define its present and desired states as part of developing a plan for reaching its outcomes. In therapeutic uses of NLP, the same process is used. Think about driving directions online: in order to understand how to get there, we first need to know where we're starting and where we want to go.

Occasionally a client will already have a desired state in mind they believe will work for them and their outcomes. If so, you can utilize that information to determine what needs to be done in order to achieve their outcome. If it doesn't work, though, you might want to find a different model (see Part 8).

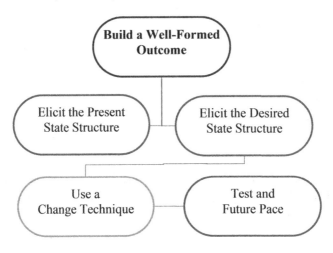

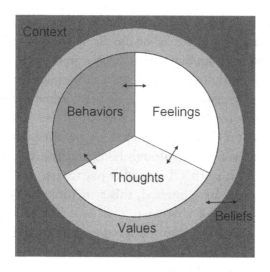

A human being is a perfect system, similar in operation to an eco-system. In the environment, every change that is made ripples out to the larger world, a phenomenon commonly referred to as the "butterfly effect." In economics, it's called the law of unintended consequences. For example, years ago in Florida land developers decided to increase the amount of buildable land by drying up some of the Everglades. They're research led them to the Melaleuca tree, a nonnative species they nevertheless planted in large numbers. Twenty years later, the plant had done its job, it had also become so overgrown that choked out indigenous plants and animals, and its bottlebrush-like flowers became a major allergen for local residents.

Every change in one part of a system will automatically affect every other part of the system.

If you have a problem behavior that needs to change in a particular context you can do so by affecting the feelings about it, the strategy that creates it, by satisfying the values in another way, or by changing your beliefs about it.

The diagram to the right shows how all these elements work together. You can see how the feelings, thoughts, and behaviors all influence each other. The values uphold those elements. Beliefs, by this model, span contexts, meaning that a belief held by an individual will be held at any time and in any place. On the other hand, values, behaviors, feelings, and thoughts are specific to certain contexts.

This system is what I like to call the snowball effect. Once a person has a thought, a feeling is likely to follow, which eventually creates a behavior or a change in physiology. And everything is fine, unless one part gets out of control.

For example, when I was attending a training course with Richard Bandler in 2004 I felt a chill in the room. It's cold in Scotland in the summer! So, I began shivering. And once that started, so did my internal dialogue. I began telling myself that it was too cold for me to pay attention or remember anything. I started making pictures of my brain freezing! I wouldn't recommend trying this, but, as you might imagine, I started feeling colder too, which made my self-talk louder and my shivering more intense. This went on for several minutes before I jumped out of my seat and went to get some hot tea. Of course, I also realized that an NLP trainer has the skills to break this type of cycle, and so I did. And all was well.

Present State Worksheet

Calibrate physiology (Posture, etc): _____
_____

Context (The situation in which the problem occurs)

Where, when, and with whom does this issue occur? _____
_____

Thoughts (The picture, sound, or feeling being accessed)

If you were to know, what is the cause of this problem? _____
_____

Accessing cue (VAKO/G): _____
_____

Internal State (The feeling being experienced)

How do you feel when x? _____
_____

External Behavior (Actions and expressions being performed)

What do you do when x? _____
_____

Criteria (Values behind the current behavior)

What stops you from already having changed x? _____
_____

And, what is important to you about that? _____
_____

Beliefs (What is true for the person about the issue)

What makes you do x? _____
_____

What does x mean to you? _____
_____

Desired State Worksheet

Calibrate physiology (Posture, etc): _____
_____

Thoughts (The picture, sound, or feeling being accessed)

How will you know you've achieved y? _____
_____

Accessing cue (VAKO/G): _____
_____

Internal State (The feeling or mental state desired)

How would you feel when y? _____
_____

External Behavior (Actions and expressions being performed)

What will you be doing when you've achieved y? _____
_____

Criteria (Values behind the desired behavior)

And, what is important to you about achieving y? _____
_____

Beliefs (What will be true for the person about the desired state)

What do you know to be true that allows you to do y? _____
_____

What does y mean to you? _____
_____

OVERCOMING RESISTANCE TO MOVING FROM THE PRESENT TO THE DESIRED STATE

Occasionally, and sadly, uncovering a client's desired state is difficult. Talking about the problem is easy, but even thinking about a solution can be like pulling teeth. In these cases, I suggest using a series of questions that motivate being open to the possibility of change. These questions point out the consequences of remaining stuck and will often nudge the client in the right direction. Of course, remember to develop rapport before doing this. For ease and clarity, I will present the questions in terms of an issue you may be dealing with.

Take a moment to answer these questions.

How would your family, friends, coworkers, and neighbors be affected by your issue? How are your behaviors causing you problems?
What are you missing, what deficiencies can you identify?
Why you want to transform this issue?
How have you been labeled by yourself or others in regards to this issue?
What would your view of higher intelligence say about this problem? Is this something you want to pass along to the next generation?

Now, after asking these questions you may feel like it's really time to make a change. So, let's start working on the desired state. Here are a few questions to get you started.

How will your family, friends, coworkers, and neighbors respond to you making this change?
What will you do differently or additionally that you wouldn't have done before?
How would you be able to stick with this new way of being?
Why is it important for you to move forward with making this change?
Who would you be if you were able achieve your outcome?
Who or what else inspires you to move forward on this? What positive impact can you make on the world by transforming this problem?

By now, you've probably got a good amount of information and motivation to make the change. So, write it all down and keep it handy. You'll learn in the next part of this book how to actually make the change.

CHAPTER 8:
STRATEGIES

Everything we do throughout our life is a series of procedures. These **strategies**, or ways of doing things, operate in every moment, from waking up in the morning to falling asleep at night, even to dreaming. We have strategies for beginning things and for ending things.

The exact definition for a strategy is a specific syntax of external and internal experience which consistently produces a specific outcome. Human experience is literally a series of internal representations. When we know the entire series of representations involved in a present/problem state, we have a better clue as to where the problem lies.

Asking "how" naturally leads to breaking down an internal process into manageable chunks, making accomplishment of your outcomes more realistic. The question "why" usually prompts rationalization and generates excuses for the present state. This tends to create a state of inertia with little inclination to re-act. You're likely to stay stuck with "why." "How" creates movement toward what you want. Most simply, strategies are how you do what you do, so when you're using NLP, focus on the process rather than the reason by asking "how' instead of "why."

You probably have some really great strategies already. Maybe you're excellent at problem solving, making good decisions, or putting people at ease. But you're likely to also have a few strategies that don't work in your best interest. You may have an irrational fear that limits your choices, a bad habit, or difficulty having compassion for others. These strategies can cause pain, limit success, and generally make life more difficult. But, there is no need to keep running these strategies! They can be changed, replaced, or expanded to give you more freedom to experience life on your terms.

NLP Practitioners learn about strategies, because they determine the structure of a person's problem or the structure of a possible solution. By integrating the following information into your practice, you'll be able to discover where the hiccup is in a person's issue. And, you can find a solution by eliciting a successful person's strategy.

In this chapter you'll learn how to structure a resourceful strategy, make changes to a problematic strategy, and how to elicit another person's strategy.

WELL FORMED STRATEGIES

Every resourceful strategy has structural elements that result in a successful outcome. First, the best strategies have well defined representations of the outcome. You need to know the purpose of running the strategy before designing it, of course. So, you'll have to use your Meta Model and information gathering questions to get to the criteria behind the desired state.

Structurally sound strategies also include at least three sensory systems – preferably visual, auditory, and kinesthetic. This gives the whole brain a chance to participate. At the same time, make sure every possible loop in the strategy is given an exit point. For example, a person with compulsive hand washing never gets the feeling of having clean hands. Without the ability to exit, this person will continue washing her hands, always looking to feel clean but never actually getting there. Some loops are natural, like a visual-kinesthetic synesthesia, where a picture produces a feeling and vice versa. However, sometimes these loops just keep going, thereby creating a difficult situation for making a decision.

Finally, good strategies include an external check after every few steps, rather than staying completely internal. For example, if a person is trying to make a buying decision but their strategy is purely based on self-talk, they can easily end up in a loop of "Should I, shouldn't I" rather than making a decision. What would work better is to include a feeling of yes or no, or better yet, an image to match these feelings with.

Well formed strategies are efficient, having the least amount of steps necessary to achieve the goal. They are logical and sequential. They include both internal and external elements, maintain the secondary gain of the problem state, and include only good feelings and consequences.

Now, beyond these structural elements there are some functional elements that also need to be considered when designing a strategy. There are three steps that must be included; a trigger, operation, and a test.

T.O.T.E. Model of Strategies

The following model was first formulated and published in "Plans and the Structure of Behavior" in 1960 by George Miller, Eugene Galanter, and Karl Pribrim. Although it is based on computer program sequencing, it gives you a very clear structure for a strategy's sequence.

The first **Test** is a **Trigger** that starts the strategy. It establishes the criteria, or the value in running the strategy, which becomes the standard of comparison for the final Test. The trigger can be in any sensory system, and it is usually set off due to some external stimulus, like a car horn or seeing an old friend. Think of a trigger as the internal response to an external event. For example, if you have a strategy for how to run a race, when the gun goes off you start to run. In this case, the external trigger is the gun, and the internal trigger could be telling yourself to go, imagining winning the race, or any number of internal thoughts. The gun going off is also called a test, because it indicates that the intent behind going through this strategy is to cross the finish line. It is a successful trigger if you actually start running when you hear it.

The trigger also lets you know when and where to use the strategy. In the above example, hearing a gun go off on a track tells you when to start running. This trigger gives you a context for running. You wouldn't normally run a race in your house, or at a restaurant. Having this particular trigger provides a forum for racing. Besides, a gun going off is usually a great trigger for running fast!

The **Operation** phase of a strategy is a series of representations and behaviors that are designed to lead to a particular outcome and take you from the trigger to the exit. To get there, you have to access a variety of information by remembering or constructing the required information. To continue with the racing example, the operation phase consists of drawing on your experience of making your legs move the fastest they can, remembering your coaching, navigating the track, and seeing the finish line. It is this set of steps that don't always follow a linear progression that leads to successful completion of the strategy.

The second **Test** is actually a comparison between the present and desired state, or a comparison between whether or not the strategy actually fulfilled its purpose. If the strategy is to run a race, did you make it to the finish line? The things being compared must be in the same representational system (comparing apples to apples). They could be images, feelings, or even some internal dialogue. If there is a match of criteria, the strategy exits, meaning if you completed the task you set out to complete, you can move on to another strategy. If there is a mismatch, and you didn't succeed, the strategy re-cycles in one of the following ways; by changing or specifying the desired outcome of the strategy, adjusting the values by changing your intent in running the strategy, or by simply accessing more information or resources to be able to complete the strategy successfully. Essentially, the test phase determines whether or not you will exit to another strategy or loop within the same one, trying a variety of tactics in order to succeed.

Lastly, a strategy should also have an **Exit**, or a way to determine how best to proceed. In the race example, if you've passed the finish line, you've passed the test phase by meeting the criteria you set up. You are free to exit, which could be celebrating or cooling down. The test phase is evaluating your experience, then deciding what to do next.

Another way of looking at the T.O.T.E. model is much simpler. The trigger tells you what strategy to run, as well as where and when. The operation phase provides you with how to do it. The test determines whether or not you completed the task, and the exit tells you what to do next.

SUMMARY OF WELL FORMED STRATEGY ELEMENTS

Let's review some important elements every strategy should include. First, every strategy should have a well-formed outcome. You can't define a strategy without first knowing what it's for. Also, a really good strategy has visual, auditory, and kinesthetic elements involved. This ensures that every part of the brain is utilized. You'll also want to make sure all the loops in the strategy have an exit. Otherwise, the strategy runs like a broken record, never getting to the point.

Additionally, make sure the strategy includes some external check points. When a strategy only relies on internal images and feelings, there isn't a way to validate whether the elements are accurate. For example, if my strategy for giving a speech only involves how I feel about my performance, I might be shocked at the actual reception. I need to check in with the audience from time to time to get their feedback.

There are also a few other considerations that help make strategies successful. One element I consider important is efficiency. If you can do something in three steps, don't take twenty. It's just too slow to be practical. It probably goes without saying, but make sure that your strategy involves only good feeling and positive consequences. If you've got a strategy that makes carrots the most alluring snack food on the planet you don't need one that makes you feel bad when you see chocolate cake.

And, of course, the most important element is effectiveness. If you work on a strategy for deciding what to eat at a restaurant (some people don't have one), you've got to test it out. Maybe you've included all the elements and it looks great on paper. You've started with a trigger of picking up the menu. Your operation involves making pictures of the food and checking how they taste and feel in your stomach. You also include an external check by asking the server for recommendations and by looking at what other tables are ordering. You're congruent about your decision, and that leads you to exit and order. But, if you test it out and don't enjoy the meal you've ordered, you probably missed out on checking your criteria for a good meal. Maybe you didn't ask the right questions, or the server isn't the best source for that information. So, look deeper, alter the strategy, and test it out again.

THE ROLE OF REPRESENTATIONAL SYSTEMS IN STRATEGIES

When designing a strategy, you may want to understand how the different representational systems will affect each step of the strategy. Here is an overview of how to use each system to its potential.

Auditory Internal (Ai) is valuable as a filing system to keep track, summarize, and categorize experience. It's also useful in the planning process, creating a commentary on information, and for drawing conclusions and making sense of the world.

The **Auditory (A)** system is useful for adding emphasis and pulling out more information. Auditory processing is much slower, as it is sequential or analog, as opposed to digital visual processing.

Visual Representations (V) can represent a large amount of information immediately and simultaneously (a picture is worth a thousand words). The Visual system is very helpful in decision making, because it allows the possibility of simultaneously viewing all possible options for comparison. It is much more difficult to do this with sounds or feelings, since those systems are more sequential.

The **Kinesthetic (K)** system has more inertia and duration than either the Visual or Auditory systems. This is partially due to the biology and chemistry of emotion. **Kinesthetic Tactile** (somatic or external sensation) and **Proprioceptive** (body's sense of movement and inner workings) help provide information about the body. **Kinesthetic Meta** (the feeling you have about a particular feeling) is the primary method of evaluating experience. For example, you could consider how you feel about being hurt.

So, now that you know how the elements involved in well formed strategies, let's take a look at what we can do with them.

WHAT YOU CAN DO WITH STRATEGIES

Strategies can be used in a variety of ways and can be likened to the executable files on your computer's hard drive. When you select an item on your desktop, a signal is sent to run the .exe file for that program. The window opens up, and your selected program begins. Even if you know nothing about computer programming, you have experienced the results numerous times.

STRATEGY ELICITATION

> **Elicitation Points**
> - Client must be associated into the experience
> - Maintain rapport
> - Pay attention to all calibration cues (eye accessing, gestures, tonality, predicates, etc)
> - Backtrack to ensure accuracy
> - Get as much information as you can!

If you want to know a person's strategy for making good decisions or playing the violin, you're going to want to master the process of strategy elicitation. When acting as a coach, you will also want to know a client's strategy for getting depression, panicking, or getting phobic. I know this seems odd, but if you know the process your client is using to get the undesired state, you'll have a better idea of how to interrupt or replace it.

Through the process of strategy elicitation you'll learn the exact internal and external steps an individual uses to perform a particular task.

THE ELICITATION PROCESS

1. Establish rapport.
2. Identify the problem state and calibrate.
3. Associate your client into the problem state by making sure they are in their own body and feeling their feelings, and set an anchor for the problem state.
   i. *"Remember a specific time when you were...Go to that first moment and experience being there."*
4. Paying attention to nonverbal communication, especially eye accessing, ask the following questions to obtain the trigger.
   i. *"How do you know when it is time to begin...?"*
   ii. *"What happens first?"*
5. Backtrack often and re-associate your client by using the anchor you set to get the operation steps.

    i. *"So you first...then what?"*
    ii. *"Then what happens?"*
6. Obtain the test phase.
    i. *"How do you know when you're finished, or when it's time to move on?"*
    ii. *"What comparisons are made?"*
7. Notate each step in as much detail as possible.
8. Test the accuracy of the strategy by running your client through the steps and calibrating their response.

STRATEGY UTILIZATION

Once a strategy has been elicited, it can be utilized by anyone desiring to create the same results. If you'd like to play golf like Tiger Woods, this is what you'll want to do! The process is completed by feeding back all the internal and external steps to an individual in the sequence in which it was elicited.

This process can also be used for both resource and problem strategies. Why would you want to utilize a problem strategy? To make sure it works, of course! If you're not sure you elicited your client's phobia strategy correctly, try it on to find out. If you have the same response, you got it right.

STRATEGY CHANGES

Basic Strategy Design Principles

- Maintain the function or purpose of the strategy.
- Intervene before a strategy gets out of control.
- Calibrate everything.
- Use submodality shifts on unpleasant feelings, pictures, sounds, etc.
- Delete any unnecessary steps after checking the ecology.
- Ensure the criteria are accessed sequentially, not simultaneously.
- Generate the least amount of change necessary to reach the desired outcome.

A major tenet of NLP strategies is that they always work perfectly, meaning they always give the same results. Many successful strategies can be made more efficient by removing extraneous steps, more thorough by adding check points, or more successful by rearranging pieces.

By making small changes to an existing strategy, you're able to leave the general structure of an already successful strategy in place without having to start from scratch. You can change the strategy by shifting, removing, or replacing the necessary representations to get to the desired state or by shifting criteria or accessing and anchoring in new resources.

Sometimes the strategy sequence isn't the real problem. Occasionally, only one element within the strategy is creating un-resourceful feelings or decisions. One specific way to change one step of a strategy is to utilize **submodalities**, which will be explained in greater detail in Chapter 9. By shifting a client's present state representation through submodalities, you affect the resulting feelings and behaviors, and, possibly, the associated beliefs. Consider having an image in your mind's eye of a very large, hairy monster running at you. Now, make the picture smaller, and shave the monster, and watch it running away. This probably changes your feelings!

STRATEGY INSTALLATION

When I first began writing this book, I was using a word processing program that turned out to be unstable. The program crashed, and my files disappeared. I don't know enough about computer programming to either elicit or change the program files. So what I decided to do was to install a new program altogether. I didn't delete the original program, I just added a new choice, which worked out great (as the completion of this book clearly shows).

Strategy installation lets you take a process that has already been elicited, utilized, and changed by you or another master of NLP and install it in yourself or your client to achieve the desired state. This doesn't replace any other strategy they've already programmed, it merely offers a new option. This is a favored technique by many in the NLP community, because any strategy can be useful in the right context. For example, I have worked with many clients that have the "see food-eat food" strategy installed. Now, you might be thinking it would be a great idea to delete that program entirely, but then you wouldn't be taking into account the ecology of that change. What if the person ended up on a deserted island? Being open to trying new foods and eating whatever was around just might be a good strategy to have there, wouldn't it?

Strategy Installation Principles

- Create what you think or feel could possibly work.
- Check your own strategy for possible application.
- Model someone else that has a really good strategy for the desired outcome.

Make sure, if you're using this option, you remember the strategy you install is only more desirable if it is easier to run and has better emotional associations than the other programs already running in the relevant context.

To do the actual installation process, point to your client's relevant eye accessing locations to install each step of the strategy in the accessing cue location that corresponds with the representational system being utilized. Make sure their eyes follow your hand, as this installs the steps in the proper locations in the brain.

For example, to install the **Motivation Strategy** outlined below, follow these steps several times to make sure the strategy is practiced.

1. Imagining the goal completed
   a. Lead eyes to your client's Visual Constructed (Vc) quadrant
   b. Have your client imagine goal fully accomplished

2. Feel as if you're already successful
   a. Lead eyes to your client's Kinesthetic (K) quadrant
   b. Generate a feeling of Yes / Excitement
3. Tell yourself to get moving on the goal
   a. Lead eyes to your client's Auditory Digital (Ad) quadrant
   b. Have client say to themselves, in their own voice, "Just do it!"
   c. Make sure they use congruent tonality

4.   Repeat all steps at least 3 times

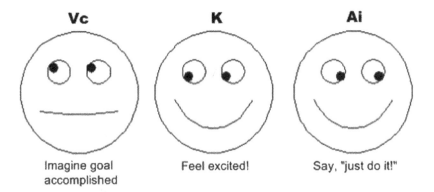

Vc	K	Ai
Imagine goal accomplished	Feel excited!	Say, "just do it!"

To install other strategies, follow the same example, changing the content and accessing cue locations. Remember to install the strategy several times in a row.

Summary

Effective information gathering is one of the most important tools a coach or consultant can have. While there are many NLP techniques for making change without specific content, most practitioners and business professionals find gathering information crucial. Let's take the example of using these techniques in a small business.

Brand X is having a difficult time. Profits are down and they are considering layoffs. Someone in human resources is smart and decides to bring in an NLP consultant. The first thing this consultant may do is interview several senior staff and a handful of employees, asking the information gathering questions and Meta Modeling the responses. Then she may gather a group together and ask further questions to determine both what the individuals believe the problem to be and what it actually is. Then she will have all the information she needs to assist the company in moving forward. Our NLP consultant will also have the tools to inspire the company to choose her methods over her competition, because she has the ability to motivate people with her language.

In this section, you've learned the types of information you need to gather in order to assist an individual or a group to move forward with their goals, how to set positive, well formed outcomes, how to uncover unconscious information with accessing cues, and how to work with strategies. In the next section you'll take what you've learned here and discover how to start making powerful behavioral shifts in yourself and others.

STUDY QUESTIONS

When I started practicing NLP, I had absolutely no idea what to do with my first client. She was 22 and an alcoholic stripper with Hepatitis C and a six-year-old son. It was a really great way to start, because I was petrified. I had no preconceived ideas of what to do. So, I sat down and began asking her questions.

Now, she was mostly coming in to stop drinking, because she knew it was making the Hepatitis C, a liver disease, worse. So I said, "When, where and with whom do you drink?" She reached into her purse and she showed me. It was 9 o'clock in the morning, and she'd already consumed half a bottle of whiskey before leaving the house. I discovered that she kept the bottle on her nightstand, and when she woke up she'd reach for it.

I also paid attention to what she was doing with her body and how she seemed to feel inside. I noticed her eye-accessing. I asked her about the role Hep C was playing in her life and what was important about keeping her current job. I asked her how she felt both while she was drinking and just before she took the first sip. I asked her why she believed she was drinking so much, and I started understanding her beliefs, until I had a complete map of her present state.

So, I had a pretty good idea of where she was, but I didn't yet know what she wanted to replace the drinking with.

1. What questions would you ask to get that information?
2. How is her current strategy notated?

If you could develop a strategy for her to achieve her desired outcome, what would it look like?

PART 3:
BEHAVIOR MODIFICATION

"Whenever we seek to avoid the responsibility for our own behavior, we do so by attempting to give that responsibility to some other individual or organization or entity. But this means we then give away our power to that entity." M. Scott Peck

INTRODUCTION:
CONDITIONING V. FREE WILL

Let's take a moment and remember Ivan Pavlov's famous experiment on classical conditioning. Pavlov was able to produce a physical and behavioral response in dogs by ringing a bell every time his dogs were presented with food. Eventually the dogs would salivate in response to the bell alone. Pavlov deduced from this that animals can be conditioned to respond to a situation in a predetermined and consistent manner.

People aren't dogs, of course, but we are conditioned to respond in analogous ways. Have you ever seen an individual in the midst of a phobic reaction? I knew a woman once that would shriek every time she saw a snake. One time I tested it out. I showed her ten snakes in ten minutes, and I got the exact same scream each time. It wasn't to torture her; I removed the phobia a few minutes later. But I wanted her to understand her response was predictable and conditioned. And if something has been conditioned, it can be reconditioned willfully.

In this section, I'll present a variety of ways to recondition behavioral responses. You'll find that, with NLP, reconditioning is simple, but very effective. You'll learn how to improve problematic steps in a person's strategy and lead them to more resourceful outcomes. You'll also discover how to use emotional states to break bad habits and develop new, positive, and compelling substitutes. Finally, you will learn how to use the values in a bad habit to motivate a person to change that behavior. It's going to be an exciting journey!

CHAPTER 9:
CHANGING BEHAVIORS USING SUBMODALITIES

When a show has low approval ratings, it usually gets cancelled. But, take a moment and think about your behaviors that have received bad reviews. How many of them have you cancelled? If you're answer is not enough, then read on.

First of all, you'll want to determine whether or not you're receiving some guilty pleasure from the behavior. Do you bite your fingernails, tap your feet, or blurt out other peoples' secrets? If so, you might have just developed a bad habit. On the other hand, if you've developed an addiction or eating disorder you probably get some positive benefit out of it.

Now, I know what you might be thinking: addictions are physical problems. Alcoholism is a disease. I don't completely disagree, but I suggest there's another component to addictions that's just as powerful, and sometimes more powerful, than the physical elements. There are many reasons a person might become addicted or develop a disorder, and this text doesn't address every single one. What I will present is the information I have used successfully with hundreds of clients over more than a decade.

There is a positive intention motivating every behavior. Human beings have needs, emotional and otherwise, and they instinctually do what it takes to satisfy those needs. If you've ever wondered why some individuals turn to crime while others don't, you can be sure it's about how they satisfy their needs. Consider someone you believe to be evil. List the behaviors they exhibit that make them evil in your eyes. Now, take a moment and step into their shoes. What might those behaviors provide emotionally for you?

Most criminals don't commit crimes because they're just hopelessly bad people. They might steal because they lost a job, or join a gang to find protection, community, or a sense of identity. Some murders are committed just for the feeling of power, or to get attention. This doesn't excuse the behavior, but it does start to explain why prisons often fail to rehabilitate inmates. If their needs aren't being met in a positive way, the same behaviors will emerge and recidivism is guaranteed.

The lesson to learn is that if you want to change a behavior you'll want to discover what it is providing. Otherwise, the pattern is likely to continue repeating itself.

There exists a context in which every behavior has value. Every behavior is useful somewhere. Consider wartime. Every country admonishes murder, but in soldiers the ability to kill is rewarded. How often are criminals recruited for military or law enforcement?

On a more therapeutic note, consider the example of the "see food" diet. Most of my clients with this approach to eating think it's bad and want it gone. But if I were on a deserted island, I'd find this to be a useful strategy. What the individuals are really looking for is to add a new eating strategy to their bag of tricks.

FIXING FAULTY STRATEGIES

In the previous section of this text, I presented three applications of strategies. In this section I'd like to address exactly how to make a strategy change. First of all, there are two categories of faulty strategies; sequence problems and submodality issues. Solving sequential problems is simple and merely requires re-ordering the steps and installing the new strategy. Submodality issues are far more common and even easier to change.

A submodality is facet of a representational system. You know we have five major modalities for experiencing the world, commonly known as the five senses, and within those sensory modalities there exist submodalities, or the qualities that make up each sense. For example, without the submodalities of size, brightness, contrast, and color, there would be no image at all. What would a sound be if it didn't have volume, speed, or tone? Submodalities are those qualities of each sense that create an actual representation.

There are submodalities within every sensory system, and the way in which they are structured determines how you feel and respond to a given representation. Imagine a small spider is sitting motionless on a rock twenty feet away. Be aware of how you feel about that spider. Now, next to it appears a six foot, hairy spider with sharp fangs and beady red eyes, and suddenly it's running quickly towards you. You probably have a different feeling about this image. But, with submodality changes, you can change how you feel about it. So, in your imagination, push that spider away and shrink it down to the size of a pinhole. Shave all its hair off, give it lavender contact lenses, and watch it scamper away. Feel better?

Such is the power of changing submodalities. In the T.O.T.E. Model of strategies, the trigger representation is the first step that sets off all the subsequent steps of the strategy. By changing the submodality distinctions of that trigger representation, you can alter the entire strategy. Here's an example. Consider a woman with a bad temper. Maybe her trigger for anger is seeing her ex-husband with his new girlfriend. Every time she sees them together (external trigger), she imagines them laughing about how horrible she is (internal trigger). That internal representation produces a feeling of anger, which builds continuously until she explodes, because she loops between seeing them and fantasizing about them wanting to hurt her.

To make a submodality change, you want to change the internal representation only. The external trigger of seeing the couple together is outside of your control. What you can do, though, is change her reaction to seeing them together. So, let's pretend I've been able to identify the current distinctions of her visual constructed (Vc) image. Let's assume the picture is a life-sized representation in full color, rolling like a movie, and it's located right in front of her face. These particular distinctions (for her, in particular) are intense and leading to her anger, so if I change them I will be able to change her response. I might tell her to shrink the picture, move it off to one side, and turn it into black and white. Eventually, we'd find the strongest driver for her emotional response, which is the submodality distinction that is having the most impact on her response. I would know when I'd found the driver, because I would be able to calibrate her body language and tonality.

There are a few tricks to successfully using submodalities. First, when working with problem strategies it's best to change the submodalities quickly so that the strategy doesn't revert to the previous format. Making the change quickly makes it more likely to be a permanent shift. So, remember to set a well formed outcome *before* making any significant changes. Also, you can use submodalities to amplify a positive feeling, as is often done while using anchoring. Anchoring is another process that can be used to change a problematic strategy.

Visual Submodalities	Auditory Submodalities	Kinesthetic Submodalities
Associated/ Dissociated	Stereo / Mono	Location in body
Color / Black & White	Location in space	Intensity
Framed / Panoramic	Volume	Moving / Still
Flat / 3D	Tone	Pressure
Moving / Still	Pitch	Area / Volume
Location	Speed	Density / Weight
Size	Clarity	Temperature
Distance in space	Duration	Texture
Shape Brightness	Tempo	Duration
Clarity		Vibration
Contrast		
Hue / Saturation		
Positive / Negative		

SOME PROBLEMS OF INTERNAL REPRESENTATIONS IN STRATEGIES

- Inappropriate or un-resourceful feelings
- Don't lead to desired outcome
- Pictures are too small to generate needed emotion
- Pictures are too large to keep emotions in check
- Sounds can be too fast , which is confusing
- Sounds can be too loud, generating too strong an emotion for desired outcome

To ensure a strategy is successful, be sure that all of the emotions are appropriate to the situation and lead to the desired outcome. Make sure all images are proportioned correctly and sounds are at the appropriate speed and volume. If these criteria are met, your strategy is likely to be successful.

CHAPTER 10:
USING EMOTION TO CHANGE BEHAVIORS

Emotional states directly affect your behaviors. If you've ever had to give a presentation to a group of peers and experienced anxiety, you're aware that your presentation skills tend to suffer. You may have stuttered, paced the room, or looked down at your feet, none of which are great behaviors to use when presenting. If, however, you came into the room feeling supremely confident and excited about the opportunity to share your ideas, you probably gave an excellent presentation. You may have made eye contact, spoke clearly, and received questions. This is because all emotional states have a corresponding physiology, referred to as a Behavioral Manifestation of an Internal Response, or **BMIR**.

You can't actually observe an emotional state in another person, but you can see its BMIR. This information is used to catch a glimpse into a person's model of the world by collecting sensory-based information. The process of collecting this sensory data and determining the person's meaning for that information is called calibration.

CONCLUSIONS ABOUT EMOTIONS

- Emotions are both in the mind and in the body.

- Emotions do not just happen to people. People have some control over how they interpret events and, as a result, some control over the emotions they experience. Emotions are choices.

• Emotions are universal. We can read other people's emotions, empathize with them, and negotiate our emotional lives together.

ANCHORING RESOURCEFUL EMOTIONS

Anchoring is the process of associating an internal response with some external trigger so the response can be quickly, and sometimes covertly, re-accessed. It has its conceptual origins in classical conditioning, developed by Ivan Pavlov and his famous dogs.

An **anchor** is simply an association, or link, between two things. The mind is literally a linking machine, and therefore, constantly links things together in order to create meaning. When we have meaning, we know how to feel about things, and know what to believe – we can operate in the world. For example, we have all learned that light switches, when flipped, cause lights to go on. We have anchored the stimulus "light switch" to the response "lights on." It can be quite surprising, in fact, if for some reason we flip the switch and the light doesn't come on. The same process also produces more pronounced behavioral responses such as road rage.

Emotions drive human behavior. Consider the times you've experienced anger. You might have shouted, used stronger language than usual, or done something else you wouldn't normally do. Emotions, which are perceived as "feelings," have a biochemical analogue, and when chemistry is altered in the brain a variety of different responses can be generated. Therefore, we can shift a problem behavior, even one caused by chemical imbalance, by shifting its corresponding emotion.

Try this at Home

This process is an excellent way to change an un-resourceful emotional anchor, thereby changing your emotional and behavior response to the external trigger.

1. Identify a behavior you wish to change.
2. Elicit your strategy for producing the behavioral response, paying particular attention to the external and internal triggers and the emotional result. See Part 2 for more details on this topic.
3. Consider which emotional response you would prefer to have in the presence of the external trigger.
4. Begin re-creating the desired emotion by bringing to mind a situation that produced that feeling in the past. Take note of the submodality distinctions of the associated visual, auditory, or kinesthetic representation.
5. Amplify the positive emotion by making the representation more compelling. If it's a picture, make it bigger, brighter, etc. If it's a sound, make it louder, put it in stereo surround, etc.
6. When the positive emotion is very strong, make a gesture that seems natural in this state.
7. While making this gesture, quickly imagine the trigger again. But this time, keep the positive emotion going as you continue making the gesture. Repeat this until you no longer need the gesture to feel good about the trigger.
8. Now, go out and test your change. Put yourself back in the situation and make sure you feel and respond differently to what used to be a negative trigger.

The resources you need to effect a change are already within you. You were born with rich internal resources, including the ability to produce emotional states, make changes to your behaviors, and form strong beliefs and values. If you're not experiencing life on your terms, you can start changing this by removing the limitations that have kept you from consciously accessing all your resources and creating the life experiences you want.

The reason anchoring works so well to change behavioral responses is that it taps your unconscious resource of emotional variety. You have the ability to produce any emotion you want. All that's needed is to attach the preferred emotion to a trigger, which could be an object, person, situation, or place. After doing this several times you will create a strong link between the emotion and the behavioral response, just as Pavlov did with his dogs.

HOW TO SET A RESOURCE ANCHOR

The process of anchoring is easy to use because you already have all the feelings you need inside you to make the changes you desire. Since emotion is chemistry triggered by a stimulus, all that's needed to recreate a previously experienced emotion is an appropriate stimulus for that particular emotion. And one of the easiest ways to do this is by reliving an experience from the past.

You've probably had the experience of driving down the road when an old song comes on the radio, and you're instantly teleported back to a specific time in your history. If so, you've experienced an anchored emotional state. In the same way, if you'd like re-create a state from the past, all you need to do is to remember a time in the past when you've had that feeling.

There are a few key concepts to creating a powerful anchor. First, the timing is crucial. You want to make sure that you catch the emotion while it is peaking or at its peak, rather than on its decline. Second, you want to ensure the stimulus is unique, meaning that it's not already strongly associated with another feeling. It's very difficult to change the emotional reaction to a hug because it's already so strongly conditioned. It would be better to use a neutral touch, word, or image. Third, the intensity of the emotion is important. If the resource feeling is weaker than the problem emotion, your work is going to backfire. Make sure you take the time to really build the resourceful emotion until it is more powerful than the problem. You can do this by changing submodalities, expanding the feelings in your body, or circulating and spinning the emotions around inside of you.

Once you have established intense feeling, you are ready to introduce your trigger. You will know you have generated the emotion in another person, because you've used your calibration skills to determine their state. You may have noticed the breathing change, color may have come into the face, and the muscles in the body may have tensed or loosened. The cues for each emotion will be different, so take the time to discover them with each client. To set the anchor, introduce your trigger at the peak of the emotional state being generated.

Keep in mind that your trigger can be in any sensory system you prefer. If you're doing this for yourself, a gesture or specific touch may be appropriate. Consider as possible anchors gently pinching your earlobe or holding the fingers of both hands together in a steeple. However, if you're doing coaching on the phone, a word or sound would work better. If you're working with someone in person, you can either use a non-threatening touch or have the client self-anchor to a specific touch or gesture.

TYPES OF ANCHORS

- Physical Touch
- Gesture
- Object
- Music
- Tone of Voice
- Space (a chair, location on the floor)
- Picture
- Smell

USING AN ANCHOR FOR POSITIVE CHANGE

Once the trigger has been set, you can utilize an anchor at any time to change a state. You can use them when you're about to take a test and need to feel relaxed and confident. You may choose to have one for giving presentations with energy and enthusiasm. Or, you might want an anchor for intense passion that you fire off every time you're with your partner. The possibilities are endless.

One possible application for using anchoring is helping children excel in school. Many children have anxieties about their performance or emotional disturbances stemming from issues at home. With anchoring, you have the ability to make positive changes in how children perform and how they feel. While not a substitute to proper education, teachers trained in NLP use anchoring to maximize standardized test scores by linking confidence and calmness to the students' pencils. Parents are also able to get their children to sleep easily by infusing "magical" objects with positive feelings. Children are very easy to anchor, because they are more freely given to imagination.

Try this at Home

Have you ever wanted to be more resourceful in a given situation? Maybe you want to be more assertive at work, or less anxious on bridges, or even more motivated to clean out the garage. Regardless of your preferences, anchoring yourself to a positive resource can help you make a positive and lasting shift in your behaviors.

This process adopted from Richard Bandler is a quick way to utilize anchoring to make this kind of change.

1. Determine the context in which you want to make a change.
2. Determine the emotional resources you need in order to respond most appropriately.
3. Access the first emotional state, and use submodalities to heighten the feeling.
4. Set a touch anchor, or use a gesture to lock in the feeling.
5. Repeat this for each resource, linking all the emotions to a single anchor.
6. Fire off the anchor, and continue to build the feelings by spinning them through your body.
7. While keeping the emotions swirling through your body, imagine being in the context where you wish to exhibit these states. Image going through the motions having this state available. Notice what you do differently, and how you feel differently.
8. Continue building the positive emotion and imagining the situation differently for another few minutes.
9. Return to the room around you, and shake off the feelings.
10. Imagine the situation again, and check how you feel about it. If it feels good, go out and test it in the real world.

ANCHORING NEW EMOTIONS

Now, sometimes there isn't a history for a particular emotion. I've had several clients want to become more confident, and nearly every time I ask them to remember a time when they were confident about something they're unsure of how to answer. Of course, I know they must have confidence in something, even if they're only confident in thinking they're not confident. But instead of fighting them on it, I find it's more elegant to use another approach, a role model.

When I first began my NLP journey I lacked confidence as a public speaker. And when I learned to do anchoring, I decided that I wanted to have the stage presence of Oprah Winfrey. I love how she commands an audience and is so calm and comfortable on stage. So, I pretended to be her, and, like magic, I began feeling more comfortable on stage!

Occasionally, it's difficult to find a suitable role model for a particular feeling, and there is no history of it either. In this case it's helpful to create the state out of the sensory representations of that experience. For example, I often have classes elicit what we call a **4-Tuple** for the state of love. I ask them what love looks like, sounds like, smells like, tastes like, and what textures and temperature love has. These answers are remarkably consistent among individuals, but it's still best to elicit them from each person. And by gathering these sensory representations of the emotions, you are able to associate into them and create the state.

Remember, to set effective anchors, be sure they fit the following criteria.

- Set at the peak of the emotion
- Use a unique trigger that will only be used in the relevant context
- Keep the state pure, so that you're only anchoring the state you desire

CHAPTER 11:
USING POSITIVE BYPRODUCTS TO CHANGE BEHAVIORS

Have you ever wondered why people do what they do? I've already invited you to look deeper into the motivations of behavior. It can be easy to get angry, or have some other emotional response, if you mistake a behavior itself for the intention behind the behavior. You'll remember from Part 2 the positive byproducts behind a given behavior reflect the value being gained from the behavior. Understanding this concept is the first step to changing an undesirable behavior into something more resourceful.

Let's take the example of overeating to discover how an intention influences behavior. Consider a time in the past when you may have eaten more than you needed. What did eating the extra amounts provide you with? While this varies from person to person, some common responses are taste, not wanting to waste the food, and getting full. But, don't rely on these answers. Discover your own instead. Let's dig a little deeper by uncovering the feelings you received from enjoying the taste, not wanting to waste, getting full, or whatever value you received. Maybe you were looking for a sense of satisfaction, pleasure, peace, love, or comfort. It is these feelings that are your positive byproducts for overeating. The process of **chunking up** to the positive intention behind a behavior was developed by Milton Erickson, and it's very useful for changing a bad habit.

WORKING WITH PARTS

Now that you understand how to chunk up to the motivating criteria behind a behavior, it's important to understand how these criteria are created and maintained. Have you ever caught yourself saying, "Well, on one hand I want to go home, but on the other a movie sounds like fun?" If so, you've experienced a "parts conflict."

A **part** is sub-personality of the mind, often created during a significant emotional experience. Usually, parts are either imprinted or modeled at a young age. Having multiple parts can increase the resourcefulness of a human being, but it creates a system of competing values that can cause conflict and indecision. Sometimes, this process of part creation results in Dissociative Identity Disorder. Chunking up to a core value, however, can often clarify the situation even in extreme cases and resolve internal and external conflicts.

For example, my parents are very different individuals. My mother has never been particularly athletic or outdoorsy, preferring to spend leisure time relaxing on a cruise or touring foreign cities. My father, on the other hand, is a bit of a daredevil. He's ridden motorcycles up Mt. Fuji, and hitchhiked across the country. Clearly, my parents have very different behaviors. Yet, if I chunk up each of their behaviors I arrive at the same value – adventure. They both crave meeting new and interesting people and places, but the way they've gone about it is very different. Still, understanding their common love of adventure, they were able to enjoy each others company, and vacation planning was usually a breeze.

In every habit or "problem" behavior there is a parts conflict. First of all, there is always a part of us that wants to do the behavior and a part that wants to stop. This conflict doesn't always occur simultaneously; often one will be stronger at a given moment in time. For example, I often get calls from prospective clients with alcohol and drug addictions. They will make an appointment, because something bad just happened. Then, a week later when it's time to come in for their appointment, they skip out. The part that's addicted has grown stronger again. Therefore, the first thing to do when dealing with a habit is to strengthen the part that wants to stop and weaken the part that doesn't. This is done through a process of leveraging the value against the behavior.

Parts are created, in response to an emotionally significant event, in order to satisfy particular needs. We have parts that keep us safe, healthy, secure, loved, and comfortable. But, some parts cease providing the benefit they were originally created to maintain. For example, I've worked with several people that began smoking cigarettes when they were in their teenage years, in an attempt to look cool and make friends. But, then 30 years later they found themselves in California, where you can't smoke anywhere in public. And if you do, people stare and make comments. Eventually the behavior of cigarette smoking stops providing the benefit of looking cool, and the individual experiences an internal conflict over the behavior.

Habits and problematic behaviors are parts still working to achieve their desired intentions long after they've exhausted their usefulness. In these cases, it's important to uncover the discrepancy between the value and behavior. Then you will be able to leverage the value against the behavior. I met a woman once on a flight to London who couldn't breathe during takeoff or landing. My astute calibration skills picked up on it right away, and I asked her what she felt holding her breath would do for her. Here's a partial transcript of how the exchange went.

Me: What do you believe holding your breath will do for you during takeoff?

Her: I don't know. I guess it's just about having something within my control.

Me: So, when you are taking off you don't feel in control? What you do feel is important about having control?

Her: Well, I know I can trust myself, but I'm not sure I can trust anyone else.

Me: So, what does not trusting people with your life do for you?

Her: It keeps me safe!

(Note: I already knew this was about safety, but leading her to find it herself was far more powerful and sustainable.)

Me: Right. Everyone wants to feel safe. But, how does holding your breath for several minutes make you safe? It seems to do the exact opposite, doesn't it?

Her: I guess you're right. I never thought about it that way before.

Me: Well, is it ok to stop holding your breath, then? If it's going to be safer for you?

Her: That sounds like a great idea.

At the end of this conversation, which lasted less than ten minutes, she fell asleep. She woke up as we were on our final descent. She was breathing normally and seemed very relaxed.

It is important to question the value and appropriateness of a behavior while maintaining the positive worth of the individual. In the practice of NLP, you'll find that people are not broken. Most clients merely do things that aren't in their best interest, which is easily changed. You'll want to make sure that you respect the individual by building rapport and separating their behaviors from the intentions behind them.

FINDING A REASONABLE SUBSTITUTION

Human beings are naturally geared towards making substitutions. Go to any Alcoholics Anonymous meeting, and you'll see what I mean. Some individuals give up drinking only to begin smoking or overeating. Others stop smoking and switch to sex. Once a behavior is stopped, a values conflict arises. A need goes unmet when the behavior is removed. And, as long as there is a need there will be a behavior to fill it. Usually the substituted behavior is no better than the original. But, if we're consciously and willfully making a substitution, let's find a way to make it a good one.

Consider a director's meeting at a large corporation. The CEO, marketing director, and finance director are present. The CEO asks each director what their plans are for the next quarter. The marketing director suggests a massive ad campaign is needed. The finance director prefers to invest last quarter's profits in buying a new building to house the growing company. The two begin to argue about which approach is best. But, the CEO, being familiar with NLP asks the directors what their plans will do for the company. Eventually, both directors come to the conclusion that their plans will either earn money or save money, and both will eventually result in stability and security for the company. And now that there is agreement, the CEO can choose an approach that will satisfy that common intention.

Try this at Home

1. Choose a behavior or habit you do that is causing some distress.
2. Ask yourself what is important about stopping the behavior.
3. Continue asking yourself the value is in making the change, until you get to a positive intention or feeling.
4. Switch gears, and begin asking yourself what you get out of keeping the habit. What is it providing for you, either emotionally or physically?
5. Keep chunking up to the positive intention by asking what value is being satisfied. You'll know you're there when you get to a positive feeling.
6. Discover what these two parts have in common. What is their common goal for you?
7. Now, ask yourself what new behavior you could create that would satisfy both the parts and the values. For example, if overeating was providing you with love, what new behavior can you add that will provide that love in a healthy and positive way?

Once two opposing parts are chunked up to their positive intention, it becomes easy to determine a new approach. No longer is the behavior itself the focus. Now, all that is necessary is generating a behavior that is resourceful and achieves the emotional or physical need.

CHAPTER 12:
CREATING NEW BEHAVIORS

Generating a new behavior from a value is quite simple. All you need to do is think up some possibilities, then imagine doing them while receiving the emotional benefit. How many ways are there to feel loved? Remember, it's not the behavior that matters to the unconscious mind; what is important is that the emotional need the behavior serves is fulfilled. Human beings are driven by emotional and physical needs, not specific actions. When you discover the need, you can change the action.

Do you exercise as often as you'd like? Have you been encouraged by your doctor to eat more vegetables? Or, do you want to develop a new routine? If so, you can easily adopt a new behavior in just a few minutes. I have consistently found that it is much easier to create a new behavior than it is to remove an old one. Since you probably didn't have much difficulty in developing bad habits, developing good habits should be just as easy.

THE THREE STEP PLAN

> ***We are the creators of our experience.***
> Occasionally it may seem that some behaviors are beyond your control. This is due to a disconnect between the conscious and unconscious minds. The unconscious mind is the part of us that maintains our habits, values, and beliefs. And, if you're unaware of the need a behavior is fulfilling, it will seem to be beyond your control.
>
> Life mastery begins when you realize that your experiences are chosen and have a positive purpose. Only then can you begin to explore that purpose and create something better. Personal power exists to the degree that you are able to take responsibility for your life and learn from it.
>
> If you're not experiencing what you want in your life, learn from it, and create something different.

Creating a new habit or behavior involves just three steps: finding a resource or role model, creating a dissociated image of doing the behavior, and installing the change by associating into the desired behavior.

Before you begin, you need to be specific and clear as to your new behavior. Remember to always well form your outcome. Then, you'll need to find a resource. In this case we're going to use a **role model** to find an appropriate strategy. Think of someone that is able to do the thing you wish to do in the way in which you want to do it. Role models are very useful resources. They provide a frame of reference, strategies, and sensory information.

If, for example, I want to learn to shoot pool, the first thing I'm going to do is find someone that does it well. I want a role model that also plays fair and for fun, because those values are important to me. I'll watch her play several times, noting her body language, eye accessing, and emotional or mental state. Soon, I'll be able to imagine her making the shots I want to make. Then I'll be able to replicate the behavior in the real world. Everything starts first in the mind.

You're imagination is one of your greatest assets. You'll find that the more you use it the more successful you are, and not just in creating positive behaviors, but in life in general. So, when you work, make sure to evaluate every change you make in the imagination first. This ensures that the change will be ecological, and it gives the unconscious mind direction.

When creating a new behavior, imagine your role model carrying out the desired behavior several times. Make sure everything about the way in which it's done fits with your values. If it doesn't, change it in your mind. I like to think of it as directing your own movie. Tell the actor what to do until they get it right.

Sometimes there are habits or behaviors you want to create for which you don't have a suitable role model. In this case, it's fine to use someone you don't personally know. You could still imagine how they would do what you want to do.

Once the movie looks good to you, it's time to take a new role. Now you'll want to be both director and actor, because you also want to be able to see yourself doing the new behavior. I can't tell you how often I've had clients tell me, "I just can't see myself doing that." When I hear those words, I know I need to help them create a dissociated image.

Association v. Dissociation

Mental note: What is the value in using association and dissociation?

Association generates feelings and installs changes. Use it when anchoring resources and as the last step in working on a change.

Dissociation removes feelings and assists in the evaluation process. Use it when considering making a change or when experiencing pain or trauma.

You have the ability to create both associated and dissociated images. A **dissociated** image is an image of yourself, and an associated image is an image from your point of view. For example, you can imagine yourself riding a rollercoaster, seeing yourself in the front seat, watching yourself scream. Or you could pretend you're actually on the roller coaster, sitting in the front seat, feeling the harness and the breeze on your face. This **associated** experience probably brings up a lot more feeling, because when you're associated you're in your body, feeling your feelings. This is where you want to be when you're using anchoring. But, it's not a great method of evaluation. Evaluating ecology is better done in a dissociated state, where you have access to more resources.

Several studies have shown that the more you rehearse a task in your imagination, the higher your performance will be on that task. Mentally rehearsing a task is equivalent to physically practicing in terms of success. So once you've watched your role model doing the task and you've seen yourself doing it successfully, then it's time to rehearse it fully associated. This installs the change at the unconscious level, making the behavior become automatic. So, step into your movie, and become the actor. Act out your desired behavior several times, feeling what it feels like to do it correctly. Now you're ready to get out in the world and use your new behavior!

GENERATING NEW BEHAVIORS IS EXPANDING CHOICES

People work perfectly and always make the best choices available to them. That is not to say that everyone always makes good choices. Human beings behave according to their needs. If I need to feel love, I have a lot of options of how to satisfy that need. And the choice I make will become a habit if it works to satisfy the need.

For example, if a 13 year old sees a group of popular kids smoking, she may decide to try a cigarette, because she wants to be popular too. Then, if that smoking behavior is rewarded by positive feedback from others she will likely continue to smoke. Now, I would suggest that smoking is not a good choice, but if the only way she can feel like part of a group is to smoke, then it is the best choice available to her to satisfy that need. But, if she were to learn NLP, she could create a new way to feel like part of the group that doesn't endanger her health.

So, if you or someone you know seems to be making harmful decisions, recognize that as it stands currently, it is the only way you might have to satisfy a particular need. But don't stop there, find a suitable replacement, and you'll expand your set of available choices.

NLP is all about pushing your limits and having more options. It's about moving beyond limitations, and there is nothing more limiting than being a victim of your habits. Add new behaviors, and apply them to appropriate situations. That way, you'll always make good choices.

SUMMARY

Behaviors and habits are easy to change and develop with NLP. Since emotions drive behavior, changing your emotional state will change how you respond. Many habits have positive intentions behind them that must be satisfied in a constructive way in order to change those habits. So, by combining anchoring with generating new, resourceful behaviors you're significantly improving your success rate.

Sometimes behaviors outlast the intentions they serve. If you're no longer having your needs fulfilled by the actions you take, consider generating a new behavior that does satisfy your emotional and physical needs. Then, all that is required is to disconnect the positive feeling from the old behavior and attach it to the new behavior. This will allow you to feel as good, if not better, about making the change. And if it feels good, you'll keep doing it!

In order to be successful in making any change, be sure to **future pace** the change. If you can't imagine having a new behavior in a particular context, then you're not likely to carry it out. Anything imagined is treated similarly by the unconscious mind to anything actually experienced. Therefore, by imagining a scenario several times the way you want it to go, you greatly increase the chances of behaving appropriately automatically in that context.

CASE STUDY: CHANGING BEHAVIORS IN CHILDREN

I work with a lot of kids with learning issues and sleep disturbances. I once had a boy I worked with for a while. He has ADHD, sensory integration problems, insomnia, and anger issues. Luckily children are easy to work with.

The main issue for this boy was insomnia. When he came in for his first session, I had just come back from a teacher's certification in Idaho, and I bought a bag of rough gem stones. I had them laid out on my table, and when he walked in he was instantly entranced by these different colored stones. I could tell he was interested, so I mentioned to him that one of the stones was made to help people sleep. I made it a game, telling him he had to guess which stone was the right one in order to take it home. So, he went through each one, checking how it felt in his hand. And wouldn't you know he actually found the one that I was thinking of!

So, I got him in a good, relaxed state and anchored that relaxation to the stone in his hand. And I told him that every time he would pick up this rock, he'd relax and fall asleep. We even had a little ceremony to activate the stone's magic, which involved imagining going into his room at night, getting comfortable in bed, and falling asleep. We rehearsed this several times. Then I told him to go home and put the stone by the bed and instructed him to touch the rock and fall asleep. His mother called me the next morning. He had fallen asleep in five minutes!

STUDY QUESTIONS

1. What are submodalities, and for what are they used?
2. What are the three main ways to change a problem behavior?
3. Consider a few ways you could use anchoring in your life. Which types of anchoring could you employ?
4. What is the difference between association and dissociation? What purpose does each serve?
5. How do you generate new behaviors?

PART 4:
HEALTH IMPROVEMENT

"Be careful about reading health books. You may die of a misprint."
Mark Twain

"The secret of health for both mind and body is not to mourn for the past,
worry about the future, or anticipate troubles, but to live in the present
moment wisely and earnestly." Buddha

INTRODUCTION:
IMPROVING HEALTH WITH NLP

"For hundreds of years, Western medicine has looked at mind and body as totally separate entities," says Herbert Benson, MD, director emeritus of the Benson-Henry Institute, "to the point where saying something 'is all in your head' implied that it was imaginary. Now we've found how changing the activity of the mind can alter the way basic genetic instructions are implemented."

Benson's Institute for Mind/Body Medicine at Massachusetts General Hospital, working in collaboration with the Genomics Center at Beth Israel Deaconess Medical Center, uncovered a connection between relaxation and the expression of genes involved with processes such as inflammation, programmed cell death and how the body handles free radicals -- molecules produced by normal metabolism that, if not appropriately neutralized, can damage cells and tissues.

But research into the mind/body connection is nothing new. In the 1970s, Robert Ader and Nicholas Cohen conducted a series of experiments on conditioning in rats. They found rats given immune suppressing drugs with added saccharin eventually experienced suppressed immune systems when given only the saccharin. In 1980, Lydia Temoshok showed that cancer patients with repressed anger had slower recovery rates than expressive patients. In 1990, Howard Hall discovered that psychological factors could directly affect cellular function in the immune system by proving an association between hypnotherapy and clinical improvements in warts and asthma, both of which can be mediated by immune changes under subconscious control. Since that time a large number of scientists have researched the links between the mind and physical health, with the consensus that a definite link exists.

While NLP is not therapy or medicine, the link between the mind and body proves that health can be improved and disease prevented by using techniques that affect mental states. NLP falls into the category of psycho-education, meaning it is a way for individuals to learn about their minds in order to make their own shifts. In the following chapters, I will introduce you to several NLP tools and techniques for reducing stress, preventing and reversing cancer, ending allergic responses, and releasing pain. Whether you want to prevent disease or desire to correct current health concerns, you have everything you need within you to create good health.

Please note that NLP is extremely useful in achieving and maintaining health, but it is not a substitute for proper medical or psychiatric care. If you or your clients have any diagnosable disorders, please seek a referral from a doctor or psychologist before proceeding with NLP. This ensures safety for all parties involved. If you're unsure whether or not a condition is a recognized disorder, please consult a doctor.

CHAPTER 13:
LETTING GO OF EMOTIONAL BAGGAGE

The link between emotions and health has been studied extensively for several decades now. Researchers like Candace Pert and Daniel Goleman have shared with the world just how important emotions are to immunity and well being.

THE ROLE OF EMOTIONS IN PHYSICAL HEALTH

The central nervous system is a huge array of connections throughout the body that allows the brain to send information throughout the body via chemicals called neuropeptides. Pioneering research by neuropharmacologist Candice Pert revealed that neuropeptides play an active role in the immune system, which is the body's defense against disease. She quotes, "Every thought, emotion, idea or belief has a neurochemical consequence."

The immune system is made up of a variety of cells that fight foreign invaders in different ways. This system is ultimately responsible for distinguishing "self" from "other," meaning it must differentiate what belongs in the body from what does not. To do this, they must travel throughout the entire body, which is relatively unique, since most cells stay in place. The neuropeptide communications from the brain must reach the immune system cells wherever they are located. But one of the more unexpected discoveries was that the immune cells themselves produce their own neuropeptides. This in effect means that a two-way communication network exists between stationary brain cells and the constantly moving immune system cells.

It is this ability to communicate with the brain that allows the cells of the immune system to trigger responses, through the brain, from the glands that secret hormones, the spleen that produces white blood cells, and the lymph nodes that eliminate waste. And the crucial link between all of these is the peptides. Peptides regulate every aspect of your body, from whether you're going to digest your food properly to whether you're going to destroy a tumor cell. It is interesting to note, therefore, that not only do changes in the rate of breathing affect the rate of peptide production, but emotions, too, can trigger their release into the body.

Furthermore, peptide receptors in the organs, endocrine muscle, and other body tissues, store emotional information received from the peptides. This creates a chemical mechanism for the storage of emotional memories in the brain and the body. And this chemical storage of emotions explains why memories and emotions sometimes surface during massage or acupuncture, and why strong emotions can overload specific areas of the body, resulting in physical responses like diarrhea or shivering. In order to remain in optimal health, your immune system needs the messages in neuropeptides balanced with the receptors' ability to receive them. And this requires your emotions to also be in balance.

LINKS BETWEEN EMOTIONAL AND PHYSICAL HEALTH

Scientists at the University of California, San Francisco, found that the stress of caring for a sick child caused cellular changes. The stressed women's cells had shorter telomeres, which are bits of DNA found at the end of chromosomes that naturally shorten as we age. The telomeres of the most stressed participants had cells that appeared about 10 years older than their chronological age. The researchers determined that chronic stress ages human cells. So, to prevent premature aging of the body, it's important to reduce stress quickly. And while it isn't always possible to eliminate the source of stress, it is possible to change your response to stressors.

In another study at the Sidney Kimmel Comprehensive Cancer Center at Johns Hopkins University, researchers determined that fear increases the likelihood of developing cancer. In this study, mice that were exposed to a psychologically stressful situation developed skin cancers more than twice as fast as mice exposed to a placebo. The researchers suggested humans could have a similar response.

Researchers at the University of California, Los Angeles published a study that indicated shame and anxiety produced greater amounts of a marker of pro-inflammatory activity. They had students write about an upsetting experience, and they found that the more shame and anxiety the participants felt, the more of this inflammatory marker their bodies produced.

STRESS AND THE IMMUNE SYSTEM

An inextricable chemical link exists between our emotions, which includes all stress in our lives, both good and bad, and the regulatory systems of the endocrine and immune systems through the central nervous system. This research emphasizes the importance of expressing our emotions both verbally and physically in an appropriate way.

When strong emotions generate fear, anger or rage, and these are not expressed in a healthy way, the body's natural response is the well-documented "fight or flight" syndrome. During periods of stress, the flood of chemical messages related to the emotions of the situation are exacerbated by the production of epinephrine, which is intended to help deal with the short term challenge. Consistent stress leads to an excess of epinephrine, which causes a chemical breakdown of the immune system cells and their communication network, and an increased potential for disease.

Anger	Fear	Sadness	Hurt	Guilt
Stomach	Throat	Lungs	Heart	Heart
Intestines	Stomach	Heart	Sexual Organs	
Colon	Legs	Large Intestine		
Liver	Spleen			
Gall Bladder	Kidneys			
	Bladder			

RELEASING DESTRUCTIVE EMOTIONS WITH NLP

In previous chapters you've learned about changing emotions using Anchoring techniques and shifting physiology. Those processes are great for changing emotional patterns and habits, and they work most of the time. However, occasionally there are traumatic experiences from the past that are continually triggered, and which don't respond to those simpler techniques. In these cases you want to have the ability to release those old stored emotions and belief systems.

Many NLPers have argued that regression techniques are unnecessary. Some believe it's the strategy that's faulty, not the memories themselves, and I agree this is true in many cases. But it can be very difficult to convince clients who have experienced painful situations that those memories aren't a problem. Most believe they need to work those issues in order to heal. And, if you're familiar with the placebo effect, you understand that working within an individual's model of the world will have greater impact.

The **placebo effect** is one of the most powerful demonstrations of the mind/body connection. Do you remember the boy I gave a magic stone? There was nothing inherently magical about that rock, but he believed it worked, and it did. Belief is more powerful than knowledge. A belief is the most powerful force I have encountered that effects an individual's model of the world. Think about it for a moment. It's beliefs that start religious wars. It's a difference in beliefs that shape our political system, our personal relationships, and our health.

For our purposes here I will define a belief as a thought paired with emotional conviction. Remember, human beings are emotional machines. We don't run on pure logic, no matter how much some individuals would like to thinks so. Neurologists use the metaphor of trying to control an elephant when you're sitting on its back to how we try to overcome emotion with reason. Emotion is just so much more powerful in our decision making process, due to emotion being an unconscious process. And when we develop beliefs it's a process of making decisions of what to believe and what to reject.

All beliefs were once decisions. For example, consider the example of a child being teased on the playground. Once the insult is hurled, the child has the option to either accept the comment as true or to reject it as false. This decision is likely to be made based on the emotional reaction, which could be positive or negative, depending on the child's age and existing beliefs. Before the age of seven, children are purely emotional. There is no critical factor in the mind that challenges comments, meaning that a young child will never ask if something is true or not. If it is said, it must have some validity. As we grow and mature we develop a critical factor and have the ability to question the world around us. Further, if a child is very sure of themselves, they may have the ability to reject a negative suggestion. This is not often the case, though. If you've ever watched kids on the playground teasing each other, you've experienced how much teasing can hurt.

You might already be familiar with hypnotic suggestion, but in case it's something new to you let's take a moment to define it. A hypnotic suggestion is any communication that gets past the critical factor in the mind. This is due to either the emotional impact it has or to the prestige of the person delivering the communication. As explained earlier, everything before age seven is a hypnotic suggestion. This is why it is so important to speak positively to children. But not only children are susceptible to suggestion; adults fall victim to it every day. Advertisers, teachers, preachers, politicians, and doctors are common sources of influential suggestion. Anyone in a position of authority or prestige has the ability to bypass the critical factor in an individual's mind. And, it should be noted that this is not necessarily a bad thing. Many of these individuals are giving positive and resourceful suggestions. However, negative suggestions can get through just as easily. These suggestions, if accepted, become limiting beliefs that affect the individual for as long as they hold the belief.

In order to permanently release negative emotions from a person's body and mind, it's important to change the beliefs that trigger the emotional response. One tried and true method for changing both the belief and the emotions connected to it is regression back to the event in which the limiting decision was made.

REGRESSION 101

Every individual has a method for separating the past, present, and future. In NLP we refer to this structure as a timeline. You may remember seeing a timeline in history books, with markers for when certain events happened. Your personal timeline might differ drastically from another person's, but everyone has one. Just like riding a people mover at Disney World, this timeline allows you to easily and gracefully move into the future. It's an excellent way for retrieving old memories and limiting beliefs, and for creating a compelling future.

When leading yourself or another individual on a timeline journey, it's important to find the root cause of the issue you're working with. The **root cause** is the earliest experience in which the limiting decision was made. There are probably several memories linked together in a **gestalt**, or a cluster of experiences linked by common emotions. Most of these other experiences filed in the same category are extraneous. If you resolve the very first experience, the others might never have happened. Yet, there are occasions where the subsequent memories also contain powerful emotion. In these cases they will also need to be resolved separately. You will know whether or not to work on those experiences based on how well the emotion is cleared after resolving the root cause.

Another important piece of the puzzle is disconnecting the emotion from the memory. We can't change what has happened to us in our lives, but we can change how we feel about those experiences. There are several ways to clear the destructive emotions from the root cause event.

GAINING LEARNING

The value in this method of clearing emotions is in providing a positive resource for future situations. By gaining learning, you add an option to your toolbox of how to respond in similar situations. This is a very powerful technique, and it's very simple to do.

This method takes advantage of two different perceptual positions, association and dissociation. You may remember that dissociation provides learning and association changes the feelings. Consider the example of a friend of mine. He was on his way to work one day, when a car exiting the highway ran a red light, plowing into him at 45 miles per hour. His car was totaled. He got out, unaware of being in shock, and talked to the police. Against their suggestions of going to the hospital, he called a cab to take him to work. About 2 hours later, when the shock of the accident wore off, he started having difficulty breathing. When he went to the restroom, he opened his shirt and discovered that his entire chest was covered in purple bruises. He borrowed a car and went to the hospital. They admitted him for a week. He'd broken nearly every rib and had internal bleeding.

The doctors told him he would suffer from arthritis and chronic pain due to his injuries. What I found interesting was that he never developed any of these lasting pain or negative effects from the accident. Once he healed, which happened very quickly, he was fine. After questioning him I realized he had done an NLP process on himself without realizing it. He told me he had a lot of time to think about the accident while lying in the hospital bed. He mentioned replaying the accident over and over again in his mind, looking at it from above (dissociation). What he eventually realized was that if he had waited three seconds the woman would have sped past him. He imagined doing that several times, mentally avoiding the accident by counting to three before hitting the gas. He decided that from that moment on he would do that at every green light.

Pain is a message, or a signal that something is wrong. By gaining positive, self learning and applying it to current and future situations, you no longer need the physical or emotional pain signals. The pain's message has been delivered and acted upon. Of course, if you revert to the old patterns of thought and action, the pain signal may return. Therefore, to create a new, more pleasant life experience, learn from your past and apply that learning by changing your behaviors.

RE-ANCHORING

By now you know the usefulness of anchoring. And, replacing the negative emotions with a positive resource in the root cause event also provides a new experience of the relevant context. Going back on a timeline and changing the feelings in the actual event purges the emotion from the body, often creating the opportunity for new learning, as explained above. When combined with gathering learning, the change is even faster and more powerful.

ELICITING HIGHER CRITERIA

Unpleasant emotions are often held on to because an individual believes it is serving them in some way. Often the way in which it's working is unconscious for the person. By chunking up the behavior or emotion to its higher criteria you'll be able to uncover why it persists.

For example, I once had a client that was very angry with her mother. She explained that her mother never loved her and was verbally abusive. When I took her back on her timeline to the root cause, she remembered being on the playground. She wanted to show her mom she could do a trick on the parallel bars. Her mom was talking to a friend and wasn't watching. My client made the decision at that moment that Mom didn't care about her. She was so angry she wasn't able to gain any positive learning, and she was resistant to re-anchoring. So, I asked her what was important about holding on to the anger. She recognized that it was keeping her from being further hurt by her mother. Ultimately she believed that anger was keeping her safe. After I asked her if there was another way to feel safe with her mother, she realized that the anger was more harmful to her. She had developed severe digestive issues, and she knew there was a connection. So, she gathered that learning and released the anger.

CHANGING SUBMODALITIES

You probably remember that by changing the submodality distinctions of a given sensory representation will change the resulting feeling. Making a submodality shift on a root cause memory is similar to changing any internal representation. There are a few distinctions we can now add to your existing list.

One common problem I find in root cause representations is a discrepancy in scale. For example, a person with a fish phobia that developed in childhood may have a picture that is too big. This could be because the child was small at the time. And even though they have grown since, the picture retains the original scale. So, make sure pictures are properly proportioned.

Another distinction that seems important is in the kinesthetic system. The location of a feeling in the body is closely linked to its interpretation and resulting belief. If someone hurls an insult at me, I might feel a sharp sensation in my heart. This feeling is interpreted as hurt, and I could develop the belief that the individual is bad. But, if I hear the insult and move the feeling to my left foot I could interpret it completely differently, and more objectively. It sounds strange, but it works!

Lastly, remember that tone of voice is very important in how we interpret a communication. Tonality is also important to shift when working with root cause events. For example, if there is a memory of your mother speaking to you in a critical tone, you could make her sound like a mouse. If any voice is creating bad feelings, change the tone.

GENERALIZATION

The final piece necessary in conducting regressions is generalization. As mentioned earlier, finding the root cause and disconnecting the negative emotions and beliefs are crucial. But, resolving the past doesn't necessarily change the future all on its own. Remember, the root cause is part of a Gestalt, and while clearing the emotion from the first event is critical, releasing the emotions from the subsequent events is a necessary step to ensure success.

As with any process you perform, you'll want to future pace the change. This aspect of generalization takes all the changes made you made in the past or present into the future. You want your client to be able to imagine responding in the future differently, and a mental representation of this is the most effective method. To future pace a change, have your client create a dissociated movie of feeling and responding in the desired way in all the relevant contexts. Then, associate the client into those experiences to really get a feel for the change. This will solidify the work you've done.

Chapter 14:
Secondary Gain and Motivation

Now that you understand the role that emotions play in determining health, let's look at another possible cause of disease and ill health. Psychosomatic conditions are physical reactions to emotional situations. It is well documented that mental and emotional factors can produce health issues that have no apparent physical cause. Often patients with a psychosomatic illness are told by their doctors that they're "making it up." I disagree. Just because there is no physical cause of an illness does not mean it is imaginary; the cause is most likely emotional, or driven by **secondary gain**.

Psychosomatic Defined

Psycho: related to the mind, psyche
Somatic: related to the body

A psychosomatic condition is a mind/body issue. The mind influences the body, and the body influences the mind. Therefore, a physical problem can be brought on by an emotional episode, and an emotional trauma can occur in response to a physical condition.

For example, stress compromises the immune system and can increase susceptibility to illness. On the reverse, physical pain can lead to depression.

Further, physical symptoms can be created by thoughts. Research on biofeedback has shown thoughts can change the body. You can slow down your heart rate, increase blood flow, and regulate digestion with your thoughts. So, isn't it also likely that certain thoughts can trigger physical illnesses?

Now, of course it's possible to create disease from thoughts and emotions. But, what about situations for which you can find no apparent cause? Consider the example of a client of mine that desperately wanted a second child. She'd been trying for a year with no success. When she came to me she was unsure that I would be able to help, because she knew that I worked with emotions. She insisted there was no emotional connection, but after asking a few questions the situation became clear.

Her first child was born shortly after her father passed away. Someone had mentioned to her that maybe the child was a gift from her father, meant to fill the hole that his passing left. When I asked how she interpreted it, she indicated that she felt that a new soul could only come in when another one left. This, as you might expect, brought forth some strong emotion, which let me know we had found the key. This belief, which had been out of her conscious awareness for a long time, coupled with the grief she had for her father created a situation of incongruence. She wanted a child, but didn't want to suffer another loss.

I consider incongruence and secondary gain to be connected. When there are two or more parts in conflict, there is a disparity between the emotional motivations. In the above example, my client had two separate parts, one that wanted a child and one that didn't want anyone else to pass away. The part that didn't want more grief provided secondary gain, or a motivation to not get pregnant. As long as that secondary gain was there, she couldn't make her body cooperate with what her conscious mind was telling it to do. When there is disparity between the conscious and unconscious motivations, the unconscious is likely to win out.

For the purposes here, I will define secondary gain as a belief or value that is driving current results. For example, one of my first clients was allergic to cats. I cleared it using a process I will share later, but it came back within a couple of weeks. So, I dug deeper and found out that he had dropped out of college to take care of his bedridden mother – and her cat! He was a little resentful of having the added burden of the cat, and so developed an allergy to have an excuse to get out of the house once in a while. Once he realized that, we worked to find another way for him to feel comfortable taking time for himself. The allergy released minutes later. In his case, his secondary gain was a value: time to himself.

How to Determine a Person's Motivation to Get Healthy

Begin by asking why the person believes they haven't healed yet. Then, ask if there are any benefits to being sick, even silly ones.

Is there something they don't have to do when they're not feeling well? Do they have to make fewer excuses for staying home or avoiding certain people? Does it give them time and space for themselves?

Other common motivations behind health concerns are attention, love, safety, and meaning, or purpose. If you've been around children, you understand the importance of attention. Every human being needs recognition and love. Without it, we fail to thrive. Babies will even die if love is withheld. It's one of the strongest needs we have, and most of us will do anything to get it, including getting sick enough to require another person's care. Needs for safety also affect health. I have seen numerous students develop fevers, colds, and other illnesses to prevent failing a test. These people are not faking it! Adults do it as well, getting sick before a presentation or interview. One motivation that is often forgotten is the need for meaning. As we age, our identity shifts from child, to adult, possibly to parent, then grandparent. But, occasionally, an individual will feel they have nothing to live for, no significance, and nothing to talk about. In these cases, becoming a patient is their new identity. This motivation is particularly dangerous, because without a healthy identity to replace the sick one, the individual's fear of the unknown is too strong to let them heal.

HOW TO WORK THROUGH SECONDARY GAIN

So, what do you do when there is an unconscious motivation that is sabotaging your plans?

There are two main ways to use secondary gain; it can be used as leverage against the issue and it can be satisfied with anchoring. In most cases I recommend anchoring, but leverage is quicker, simpler, and can always be used first. If it's not fully successful, you can still follow up with anchoring. For this reason, I'll explain leverage first then show how to use them both together.

USING CRITERIA AS LEVERAGE

The secondary gain behind a health issue, or even a habit, can be used to provide leverage against keeping the problem. Secondary gain exists to avoid pain, but it usually serves to create more of the problem than it solves. You can use this knowledge to leverage against your client's resistance to change. For example, if someone has developed an allergy to dust, and they despise vacuuming, you can guarantee there is secondary gain involved. So, you'd have to chunk up to get the positive intention behind the allergy. Here is an example.

So, what does this allergy keep you from doing that you really don't like doing anyway?
Well, I don't have to vacuum.

Do you like vacuuming?
Not at all!

Ok, so you get to avoid that. How does avoiding vacuuming really serve you?
It gives me time to do something fun, like taking a hike or playing with my dog.

Great, so you get to have fun. But, I have to ask, is it fun to live with all that sneezing and sniffling?
Of course not!

Then, let's release the allergy so you can truly have fun and feel good.

In this example, the secondary gain, or motivation, behind the allergy is having fun. And I've used that information to show how the allergy isn't fun. In the process I satisfied the secondary gain by showing it was possible to have fun without the allergy.

USING ANCHORING TO SATISFY MOTIVATING CRITERIA

If the client is still resistant to letting go of the problem, which is often evident in their nonverbal communication or in the results of your work, you'll want to anchor the positive intention and apply it to the relevant context or situation. The process is the same as noted above, with an addition two steps. Here is an example.

So, what does this allergy keep you from doing that you really don't like doing anyway?
Well, I don't have to vacuum.

Do you like vacuuming?
Not at all!

Ok, so you get to avoid that. How does avoiding vacuuming really serve you?
It gives me time to do something fun, like taking a hike or playing with my dog.
Great, so you get to have fun. So, let's pretend you're playing with your dog now. It's fun, right?

(Set an anchor for the feeling of fun. Fire it off while you introduce the vacuum.)

Now, pretend you're having fun with your dog, while you switch the picture to a vacuum. See how much fun it can be to vacuum?

Keep switching between the pictures, intensifying the feeling of fun. Eventually the client will associate the vacuum with the feeling of fun, and the unconscious resistance to vacuuming will be removed. Then you're free to remove the allergy.

CHAPTER 15:
WORKING WITH WEIGHT ISSUES

There is a lot of disagreement about the best way to lose weight. One thing is for sure; it is pretty much agreed that diets don't work. When it comes to losing weight, there are several factors that need to be addressed.

- The cause(s) of the weight
- Secondary gain of being overweight
- Compulsions
- Body image

First, you need to determine the main contributors to the current weight. Is your client overeating, too sedentary, too stressed, or choosing the wrong foods? Overeating is a common issue, but it's not the only possibility. Some individuals feel compelled to eat certain high calorie foods, and they need to break that addiction. Other people hold onto weight because of high stress in their lives. Still others lack the motivation to exercise. For most individuals, there are a variety of factors that need to be addressed.

CAUSES OF OVERWEIGHT

OVEREATING

When individuals overeat, there are two forces at work. At times it is merely an issue of eating too fast and not being able to receive the signal from the brain that says, "I'm full." In these cases, creating a slower eating behavior is extremely helpful. The other contributor to overeating is more complex, as it involves emotional eating. Some individuals experience deep and painful emotions, and they have become addicted to food. They seek to fill a void in their lives with food, which only works temporarily. Once the food is digested, the pain returns, thus creating a vicious cycle of eating and hurting. This can be compounded by feeling guilty about overeating.

Determining the cause of a person's overeating is simple. If the person is obese, there is almost certainly an emotional component. It is reasonable to expect an individual to gain a little weight by eating too fast, but this won't create long term, excessive weight gain.

EMOTIONAL EATING

If you even suspect an emotional cause, make sure you address it by conducting a regression to the root cause of the emotional void. Or, regress the client to the moment they linked food to the emotion.

UNCONSCIOUS EATING

Unconscious eating is one of the major contributors to overweight. Individuals that suffer from this condition often are completely unaware of how much or how often they are eating. They may even "zone out" while eating, or will find themselves staring into the fridge without knowing why. Some extreme cases even involve night eating, which is similar to sleep walking. These people will get up in the middle of the night, sometimes completely unaware they are up, and will eat very large quantities of food. One possible cause of night eating is the use of antidepressants.

Unconscious eating, while challenging, can be changed by working with the part of the mind that feels compelled to eat. Once the higher value is satisfied with another behavior, you can install a new strategy that includes checking hunger before eating.

Whether your client is an emotional or unconscious eater, you'll need to find out what emotional needs are being met by overeating. This is done by chunking up the parts involved to the positive intention they serve. Then, you can find another behavior that will satisfy that value, or intent, and use the Behavior Generating process from Part 3. Anchor the feeling, and attach it to drinking water, eating slowly, or anything reasonable. Then future pace that change, dissociated first, then associated. Fire off the anchor in all the relevant contexts.

STRESS

When you're under stress and a fight or flight response is triggered, the body releases a hormone called cortisol. When cortisol is released into the body, it lowers your metabolism to conserve energy. Naturally, if you experience chronic stress leading to elevated cortisol, your metabolism is constantly low. This results in fat accumulation.

Other ways stress links to weight gain is that it affects food choices, fat storage, and blood sugar fluctuations. Often when people are stressed they crave crunchy, salty, and sweet foods. They may also opt for fast food instead of a home cooked meal. Unfortunately, these foods tend to be high calorie foods. Prolonged stress can also change your blood sugar levels, resulting in diabetes and fatigue. Fatigue usually results in less physical activity, making burning calories more difficult. Stress is also linked to greater amounts of abdominal fat.

For details on reducing stress, see Part 8.

LACK OF EXERCISE

Of course, any successful weight loss program needs to involve physical activity. Research is conclusive; a healthy diet combined with moderate exercise is the best way to lose weight. It's necessary to burn more calories than you ingest in order to lose weight, and most everyone knows this. The problem is that many individuals lack the motivation or are too fatigued to get the necessary amounts of exercise to reach their target weight.

In order to assist someone in getting enough exercise, you'll need to discover what's holding them back. For some it's stress, for others it's the fear of being humiliated at the gym. In either case, my favorite process for this is Milton Erickson's As If Frame.

Try this at Home

1. Pretend for a few moments that it's been 6 months or a year, and you've successfully reached your ideal weight. Your body is toned, slim, and full of energy.
2. Check yourself out in the mirror. Take in how good you look.
3. Feel what its like to have this body. How much energy do you have? Do you feel lighter, more confident?
4. How do the people around you act towards you now? What have you heard from others lately?
5. Now that you've done it, and you can see and feel the results, think back over your process. Ask yourself the following questions.
   a. How did you motivate yourself to exercise?
   b. How did you stay motivated, even when it was a challenge?
   c. Did you work out with someone or by yourself?
   d. What other changes did you make that led to your success?
   e. If you had the opportunity to teach someone else how to do what you did, what would you share? Why were you successful?
6. Now, reorient yourself back to the present moment. Imagine implementing everything you just learned immediately. See yourself going through all the motions, exercising, and making all the necessary changes. Watch yourself getting results.
7. Then, step in to that image and feel what it feels like to get the exercise. Pay attention to how good you feel when you're done. Rehearse doing everything just as you set up three to four times. Make sure you do it consistently and for long enough!
8. Bring yourself back to the room, anchor the good feelings, and remember to fire off that feeling every time you need a boost.

SECONDARY GAIN AND OVERWEIGHT

There are many hidden benefits to being overweight. Some women, in particular, put on weight to keep them safe. Many of these women have suffered sexual abuse in the past, and they believe that being overweight makes them unattractive. Therefore, they feel they will be safe if they are overweight. Some people might use their weight to keep them safe from rejection. They find it easier to blame their weight for problems, rather than looking deeper into the real reasons for their lack of success in relationships or at work. Still others have a false belief that being physically bigger makes them safer, when in fact it's more of a health risk. I have even had clients that held their weight to feel powerful. They believed that by occupying a larger space, they would get more attention. Unfortunately, the quality of the attention didn't match up with what they desired.

Boredom is another consideration. Many individuals eat to fill time and loneliness. In order to correct this behavior, you'll need to generate a new way to fill the space that food fills. Consider replacing this behavior with taking a short walk, doing a few sit ups, or doing a five minute meditation. Another possibility is to use an anchor to dissolve the bored and lonely feelings. This may be the best option in most cases.

As you can see, there is a variety of motivations behind overweight. Now, this is not to say that every individual that is overweight has secondary gain. But, I bet if you dig deep enough you'll find some small motivation in nearly everyone. Keep in mind, this is usually outside of their conscious awareness and will have to be uncovered carefully.

Another important note about secondary gain in regard to weight is that there can be different motivating criteria for being overweight than there is for overeating. For example, an individual might feel compelled to overeat to reduce stress and produce a food coma, but that person may stay overweight because she feels more powerful being bigger. These multiple layers of secondary gain need to be addressed separately and completely for long term success.

COMPULSIONS

Have you ever met anyone with a see-food diet? I have a friend that will instantly grab a chocolate in front of her without even thinking about it. For her, eating chocolate is a compulsion. She can't not eat it. It's similar to someone that bites their nails or twirls their hair. If you move their hands away, they move back immediately. It seems to be beyond control, and to some extent, it is.

Luckily, compulsions can be changed with NLP. Keep in mind, if an individual can develop one compulsion, they have the ability to create another one that's healthier and more sustainable. In NLP terms, a compulsion is a strategy. Most compulsion strategies are very similar in structure. They start with a trigger, often seeing or smelling food, in this case, then move to a very strong positive feeling. The result is a movement towards the food. Remember, the simplest strategies are the most effective.

Changing a compulsion is as simple as replacing the food the person is compelled to eat with something healthier and lower in calories. This is done by attaching the feelings produced by chocolate, as in the above example, to carrots, for instance (hard to believe, but it works). Then, you can disconnect the strong feeling attached to the chocolate by distorting the internal representation. In other words, you'll be using submodality changes to shift the compulsion.

Try this at Home

1. Specify what you're compelled to eat. Bring to mind your internal representation of that food. If it's a picture, what does it look like? If it's a smell, note the power of the odor. Create an image from the smell.

2. Find a suitable replacement. Some suggestions are baby carrots, celery, or a glass of water.

3. Create a representation of that food in the same sensory system as the food you're compelled to eat. Match the submodality distinctions of the replacement to the compulsion.

4. Now, imagine how a slideshow transitions from photo to photo. Maybe it fades to black, turns a page, etc.

5. Bring the compulsion picture into your visual field. Get the feelings of compulsion, just as you transition to the healthy picture. Do this fast.

6. Blank the screen in your mind and repeat step 5 several times. Blank the screen each time.

7. To finish, anchor a feeling of strength and power. Then bring the unhealthy picture back for a moment while firing off the anchor. Then, shrink the image and push it away very quickly.

BODY IMAGE

Another very important consideration when working with weight issues is body image. Commonly, individuals with eating disorders and weight problems have distorted body images. The TV show *How to Look Good Naked* illustrated this by having an overweight woman select her correct belt size from a variety of options. As you may expect, she chose one much larger than her actual size. This has been repeated with a number of individuals in a variety of ways. I had a client a few years ago that had been overweight for about 20 years before realizing it. She only recognized it when she attempted to put on a skirt she hadn't worn in that long, and it didn't fit. Suddenly, she looked in the mirror and saw herself for the first time.

How many people have accurate self images? Not too many, in my opinion, have perfectly realistic self concepts. This could be due to the thousands of times we have seen ourselves. These images overlap over time, blurring our image of who we are. And this is not to say that an entirely accurate self image is necessary. However, something close to realistic is helpful. The trick, though, is to have good feelings attached to that representation, no matter how big or small you are.

Many years ago, I worked with a group of teenagers with body image issues. I gave them each a large roll of paper they could use to draw themselves as they believed they were. Then, I had them lie down on top of the image while someone traced their real shape over the top. The results were astounding. Every teen drew herself larger than she actually was. Even the proportions were off. Once they saw themselves as they were, they started feeling better about their size and shape.

EATING DISORDERS

There are three types of eating disorders that involve body image issues: anorexia, bulimia, and body dysmorphia. *Anorexia Nervosa* is characterized by extreme dieting, starvation, and a distorted body image. Anorexics see themselves as much larger than they are, and they often wear baggy clothing that reflects this discrepancy. They also often have a phobia of gaining weight. *Bulimia Nervosa* is characterized by extreme control issues, often resulting in purging, excessive exercise, and taking medications to control weight. Bulimics see themselves as imperfect, and so are often seeking perfection through self control. Body dysmorphia is the psychological term for distortion in body image. Muscle dysmorphia occurs most often in men, indicated by dissatisfaction with the size and definition of the musculature of the body.

While these disorders are beyond an NLP Practitioner's scope of practice, you may run across them in your work. In some instances you may choose to work alongside a psychologist on these issues. There are a few considerations to take note of in working with eating disorders and body image.

There are several aspects to these issues that need to be addressed.

- Body image
- The particular cause of the weight
- Emotional connections to food
- Guilt and self punishment

- Need for control

- Obsessions and compulsions

First is the actual distorted body image. This is best done by using a reality strategy as described above. Secondly, there is often an obsession with physical appearance. You will need to shift this using the values change process explained below (you'll need to substitute healthy food for physical appearance). A third issue to consider is self punishment. Some people find that overeating, or eating at all in the case of anorexics, creates a feeling of guilt. This guilt usually results in self punishing behavior like starving, purging, excessive exercise, or taking medications. Resolving this guilt is essential for long term success in overcoming eating disorders.

HOW TO STAY SLIM, NATURALLY

It is possible to eat what you want, when you want it and still stay slim and fit. There is a trick to it, though. Individuals that seem to be naturally slim have the following things in common:

- Naturally slim people generally eat only when they are physically hungry. They don't eat because they have a craving, emotional upset, or because they're bored. If they do eat when they aren't hungry, it is usually just a taste or two.

- Naturally thin people have a strong rapport with their bodies. They are able to follow the guidance they are given by their bodies, including being able to stop eating when they're full. They find it easy to distinguish between a signal from the brain and one from the stomach.

- People who stay slim have a sense of what healthy foods look like, and they find their taste satisfying.

- Naturally thin individuals consider health to be a very high value in regards to food. It's usually a higher value than taste, but both are on the list. Feeling good is also a common value in this context, and naturally slim people believe that healthy food will make them feel better.

- Slim people don't need to satisfy their needs immediately. They will consider the effect of their actions before taking action.

Now, you might be thinking that this isn't your pattern. However, your pattern can be changed. All of these criteria can be developed using NLP. The first step is to develop a rapport with the body, especially the stomach, which can be done in several ways including "talking" to your stomach, taking the time to check in with your physical and emotional feelings before eating, and deep hypnosis. I find that tracking your eating patterns is the most effective. By paying attention to when you eat, what you're feeling just prior to eating, and in what situations you tend to overeat, you develop a sense of your pattern. Then you can eliminate the eating that doesn't match with a rumble in your tummy.

Values Shift Process

Valuing health above taste is a very useful step in becoming naturally slim. It doesn't require you to ignore taste altogether, it simply makes health more important.

1. Think of your favorite unhealthy food, and access your representation of it. Elicit the submodalities of the image.
2. Ask yourself what benefit you receive from eating that food.
3. Bring into consciousness your representation of healthy food, and elicit the submodalities.
4. Knowing that a main motivator in eating healthy is to be slim, ask yourself why you don't eat healthy now.
5. Consider a situation in which that reason is invalid. For example, if you don't eat healthy because you don't have time to cook, consider something that you'd make time for, no matter what. Ask yourself what value is being satisfied by that.
6. Imagine how that value can be satisfied even easier by eating healthy foods.
7. Shift the submodalities of #1 with those of #3, and vice versa, keeping the content the same, so that #1 now looks like #3 and #3 looks like #1.

The second step in developing a strategy for staying slim is to begin craving healthy foods. Now that you understand anchoring, this should be easy. Simply anchor the feeling of liking or craving, and link it to a variety of healthy foods that you want to like. Then, anchor the feeling of dislike and link it to the unhealthy foods you crave. Keep this anchor so that you can use it when you're in a situation where you start craving something unhealthy. Eventually you'll find your preferences will change naturally.

One of the most important stages in becoming naturally slim is to rearrange your values in regards to food. When you value something, you'll do whatever it takes to satisfy that value. Therefore, it's a very powerful change and should be respected as such. The Values Shift Process I've developed is one of the fastest and most powerful ways to make health a more important value in your life. It isn't to be taken lightly, because it will affect all of your behaviors in that context.

Finally, timing is a crucial element in developing the body and health you desire. A naturally slender individual is more likely to choose foods that will make them feel better *after* they've eaten them, not *while* they're eating them. They will consider the long term effects of the foods, not just the immediate satiation of hunger or taste. So, the next time you have to make a food decision, ask yourself what you could eat that will leave you feeling healthy and satisfied in thirty minutes. You may be surprised by the answer!

CHAPTER 16:
CLEARING ALLERGIES, HIVES, AND ASTHMA

I have found NLP to be profoundly successful in working with allergies and allergy-related illness like hives and asthma. The reason for this, I believe, is that these conditions are caused by stress. When you experience stress, your body reacts to the stress by overreacting, creating what could be called a phobia of the immune system.

What are T cells?

T Helper cells (TH) are lymphocytes, but they act very differently from most white blood cells. They don't have the capacity to destroy pathogens, they are messengers and helpers. They communicate with the immune system and determine the best course of action in the presence of an invader.

The T cells determine whether or not to release histamine or other chemicals to deal with pathogens. So, if you're able to influence the T cells, you're able to stop an allergic reaction.

WHAT CAUSES ALLERGIES?

If you have any allergies, take a moment and think back to the first time you experienced the symptoms. Bring to mind what you were going through at that time in your life. Were there any major events going on? I've found that a majority of individuals can trace the onset of symptoms to a significant emotional event, like a birth, death, career change, school change, relocation, or wedding. These events occupy our minds and our emotions, putting our immune systems on alert. And when this occurs, there is a change of command.

When you're healthy and relaxed, your immune system sends cells, called macrophages, through the body to clean up anything that does not belong. Macrophages are scavengers, sweeping your system clean, removing pollen, dust, dead cells, and other non-harmful debris. Once a macrophage has engulfed a particle, it creates an antigen, which is sent to the relevant helper T cell for cataloging. The immune system stores this information so that when the allergen is reintroduced into the blood stream, the appropriate action is taken.

In a healthy immune system, these antibodies will produce a neutral response to allergens. However, when the body becomes stressed, the immune system panics and releases histamine, which is also bound to the T helper cells. If you've ever had an allergic reaction, you're familiar with histamine. A natural result of histamine in the blood system is itchy, watery eyes, sneezing, and sinus distress.

Some researchers believe that there is a genetic predisposition to allergies, while others promote environmental and emotional causes. In either case, the immune system becomes either allergy prone (TH2) or non-allergy prone (TH1) in response to a variety of factors. TH1 immunity is good for fighting bacteria and viruses, and protecting against allergies. TH2 immunity is good at fighting parasite infections, but makes you more vulnerable to develop allergies. A healthy immune system is balanced between TH1 and TH2 immunity.

While researchers disagree on exactly what causes a switch to TH2 dominance, it is generally accepted that boosting the immune system makes it easier for it to shift back to TH1. This can be done with adequate nutrition, medication, and by reducing stress. In earlier chapters, you learned the importance of communication between the cells. Now let's also look at how relaxation can aid this communication and boost your immune system.

CLEARING ALLERGIES WITH NLP

There are three parts to working with allergies. First, you need to check for secondary gain or positive intentions behind maintaining the allergy. Second, the immune system needs to get the message to relax. Allergies are produced by hypersensitivity, and deep relaxation will correct this. Lastly, you need to create better communication between the mind and body. The immune system needs to understand that it's safe to calm down, and it requires visualization in order to know how best to proceed. You already know how to discover and remove secondary gain, so for now, let's focus on relaxation and communication.

When I work with allergies, I find it useful to explain the immune system to my clients. It gives them a frame of reference, so that they understand what it is we're doing. And to summarize, we are merely sending a message to the immune system to stop overreacting to the allergen. We're going to do this by inducing a light hypnotic state and using visualization techniques to set the intention for staying relaxed and clear in the presence of what used to be the allergen.

I once co-taught a class in Hawaii, and the weather was so nice we didn't want to be inside. So, we rented a van and drove to the North Shore, set up some umbrellas, and had class on the sand. Within a few minutes I began to itch. I looked down at my feet and saw little red bumps everywhere. When I realized I also had them on my arms, it was clear I was reacting to something. Not knowing the source of the reaction, I had to get creative. Then, I remembered a story Richard Bandler told me about overcoming his allergy to onions and decided I could use a similar process. So, I closed my eyes and focused on my breathing. I relaxed my shoulders and went into a light trance. I deepened my state by using a specific internal representation of hypnosis that I've cultivated over time. It acts as an anchor that I use regularly. Once I achieved a deep relaxation, I imagined walking along the North Shore, watching the surfers, listening to the waves, and feeling the sand between my toes. Then, I imagined lying down on the sand, feeling very calm and comfortable until I got up and left for my hotel. I imagined looking at my skin and seeing it very smooth and tan. And, I instructed my unconscious mind to go through my body and clean up the histamine (it can do this). Then I brought myself back to normal consciousness to discover the bumps had greatly subsided. By the next day they were gone completely.

It was a simple process, and it really only took fifteen minutes to complete. I've never had a reaction like that again, either. The combination of relaxation and visualization is very powerful. But what if you aren't yet skilled in self hypnosis? You can use the process below as an alternative. Or, jump ahead to Chapter 17 and read up on hypnosis.

Try this at Home

1. Elicit any secondary gain in regards to your allergy. Then, prove to yourself that it's better to live without the allergy. Get help if you need it.
2. Pretend you're in the presence of your allergen. Note if you start to have any physiological reactions to imagining it.
3. Take a deep breath, and clear your system of that feeling.
4. Bring to mind something that looks like your allergen but that is harmless to you. Make sure it looks nearly identical (pollen may look like dried mustard or flour, for example).
5. Anchor yourself to a feeling of relaxation. You could recreate a past memory, or use submodality changes to change your internal representations to something more relaxing.
6. Now dissociate, seeing yourself on a movie screen feeling relaxed with the "allergy substitute." Fire off the relaxation anchor, and keep making it stronger.
7. When you feel very relaxed, watch the substitute change into the allergen. Make sure to stay very relaxed, while you watch yourself reacting positively to the former allergen.
8. Finally, associate into yourself, still firing off the relaxation, and pretend you're in the presence of the allergen. Imagine feeling wonderful and calm, while you experience your immune system shifting to TH1.

Working with Asthma

Asthma is a chronic condition affecting the respiratory system. During the course of an asthma attack, airways are constricted by an inflammation in the bronchial tubes, reducing the flow of oxygen coming to the lungs. Both symptoms and severity can vary from person to person.

Asthma can be triggered by a number of factors. Allergens, exercise, humidity, and extreme temperatures are common triggers, but anxiety and stress are also possible culprits. Therefore, generating more relaxation with hypnosis can prevent an attack. There are also NLP strategies that can stop an individual from panicking during an asthma attack.

It is important to remember that NLP doesn't cure asthma. We are merely offering a way to manage symptoms. And one of the best ways to do so is by re-anchoring the asthma triggers. If you have severe allergies, work to clear those first. If it's more driven by anxiety, work to resolve that by anchoring relaxation and by shifting to a more positive imagined future.

I have successfully used the allergy relief process with asthma several times in the past. I find it works best with allergy triggers. Anxiety driven asthma attacks seem to respond better to hypnosis, which is explained in greater detail in Section 5.

Summary

One of the most significant discoveries in medicine is the mind/body link. This connection has shown that health is as much directed by mental and emotional experiences as it is by germs, disease, and injury. This recognition is changing how we approach wellness. The emphasis is slowly shifting to prevention rather than treatment, and this creates more space for NLP practitioners in the market place.

I think of most of the work I do in NLP to be preventive medicine. Every emotional shift I make with someone could potentially ward off an illness or disease. Every limiting behavior that's removed makes it more likely that an individual will make better choices, not just in that area, but in life in general.

So, whether or not you choose to work specifically on health related issues you are heading in that direction. So, learn all these NLP skills for yourself and your clients, and better health is likely to result.

Study Questions

1. Why is it important to resolve destructive emotional patterns?
2. What are the 4 main tools used to resolve traumatic memories and release negative emotions?
3. What role does secondary gain play in health and wellness?
4. What are two processes that are used to resolve secondary gain?
5. Name a few commonalities among naturally slim individuals.
6. How are allergies created, and how can you release their symptoms without drugs?

PART 5:
CONVERSATIONAL HYPNOSIS AND THE LANGUAGE OF CHANGE

"The purpose of hypnosis as a therapeutic technique is to help you understand and gain more control over your behavior, emotions or physical well-being."
-The Mayo Clinic 12/03

"Everything can be taken away from a man but one thing: the last of the human freedoms -- to choose one's attitude in any given set of circumstances, to choose one's own way." Viktor Frankl

INTRODUCTION:
CONVERSATIONAL HYPNOSIS

Have you ever wondered why some people are more influential than others? Some individuals seem to have a knack for getting others to listen to their ideas, buy their products, or inspire them to a particular cause. Any good NLP practitioner, hypnotherapist, coach, or business professional is able to influence others in a positive way. In fact, the ability to persuade is what these individuals all have in common. And, fortunately, it can be learned.

In this section, I'm going to present the language of influence. I should say right from the beginning that this is not about manipulation or coercion. It's about learning how to influence others in a positive and meaningful way, helping them to make the changes they want to make or buy the products and services that will make their lives easier. As with any technique, this information is best used with integrity and rapport.

The language patterns I'll cover in this section are based on the work of Milton H. Erickson. Dr. Erickson was unique as a therapist, and he's well known for being able to hypnotize even the most resistant individuals and get them to make positive shifts in their lives, which reflected in their health. The reason I consider his work to be the language of change is that Dr. Erickson was often able to facilitate these significant shifts through what is known as Conversational Hypnosis. The way in which he delivered suggestions and commands was indirect, and the client wasn't always aware of being in a trance. This method is useful when working with clients over the phone, where formal trance inductions aren't necessarily appropriate. These language patterns can also be used in the sales environment for the same reasons.

CHAPTER 17:
WHY CONVERSATIONAL HYPNOSIS IS CRITICAL TO YOUR WORK

The main objective in using **conversational hypnosis** is to bypass conscious resistance. Every individual develops protective barriers in certain contexts, and these are not always useful. Some people have barriers to spending money, others have rules about listening to different points of view, and a few have barriers to telling the truth. In any case, conversational hypnosis offers a method for bypassing this resistance in order to move forward in the communication.

Have you ever had difficulty in selling your ideas, getting an important meeting, or separating the truth from a lie? If so, you didn't know how to use conversational hypnosis. But if you've ever seen *Star Wars* (the Jedi "mind trick") or, more recently, *The Mentalist*, then you've seen conversational hypnosis use specific techniques to bypass the critical factor with normal speech.

Of course, conversational hypnosis is not as dramatic as on TV. Rather, it is a series of strategies, language patterns, and techniques that can influence others in a generally predictable manner. It isn't easy, but it can be mastered with practice. In time, conversational hypnosis can be used by sales professionals to bypass a customer's resistance to buying products and services they want or need. It can be used in law to direct a witness to tell the truth, or to influence a jury. It is commonly used by NLP practitioners to change a client's limiting beliefs or provide motivation to complete a goal. Another interesting application is in leadership (and parenting), where these methods can inspire teamwork, compliance, and motivation. Essentially, if you need to be more influential, this is the information you want to know.

HOW DOES CONVERSATIONAL HYPNOSIS WORK?

The principles of conversational hypnosis were first conceived by the great hypnotist and psychotherapist Milton Erickson. Erickson believed that trance states were not rare occurrences that had to be elaborately induced, because people slip into trance states several times a day, when they are waiting for a bus or concentrating very hard on something.

Erickson also theorized that directly trying to induce a trance state in someone or trying to give direct suggestions might lead to resistance. He preferred to use rapport, indirect suggestions, and confusion to induce trance states and influence compliance. These methods, combined with specific language patterns, create a trance in which suggestion is taken.

The first step in conversational hypnosis is creating a rapport with the subject. You've already learned that this is primarily done with nonverbal mirroring and matching. However, when doing conversational hypnosis, it also means initially agreeing with your subject. For instance, if the subject says, "I don't have the money right now," the proper response is, "You're right. You don't have the money now." Of course, you'll eventually offer the subject a solution, but you've got to have rapport first before he will listen to you.

The next step in conversational hypnosis is to confuse the issue. This is often done with language patterns referred to as Sleight of Mouth, explained in detail in Part 7. Sometimes a simple question works. "But even if you don't have the money now, can you be absolutely sure that a creative solution won't pop into your mind in the next minute or so?"

Because the nature of resistance is argumentative, another technique used to create confusion in conversational hypnosis is to encourage resistance, perhaps by saying, "No one could solve that problem. It's simply too difficult to come up with the money. There's absolutely no way you could afford this. You're going to have to go home empty handed." At some point, the subject will probably start arguing with you that the problem is not so unsolvable after all. The point is the resistant part of them just wanted to argue.

Another confusion technique often employed is to suggest the subject do more of something that isn't working. For instance, an obese subject might be encouraged to gain weight, in the effort to suggest he has control over the weight.

The final step in conversational hypnosis is to make an indirect suggestion such as, "You're not feeling as poor now, are you?" or "I'm not sure why, but it seems to me you look more excited than you did a few minutes ago." This type of indirect suggestion gets the subject focused on the positive, making it more likely they will continue on that track.

Now that you've got an overview of what you're about to learn, let's get into the details.

Chapter 18:
Fundamentals of Ericksonian
Hypnosis

Richard Bandler and John Grinder modeled Milton Erickson in the mid 1970s. They wanted to discover how he was able to produce such profound and lasting results with his clients. The results of this modeling became The Milton Model, a set of indirect language patterns that are influential, even when the listener is not in a hypnotic state. Some Milton Model patterns even evoke a hypnotic state. For this reason, Ericksonian Hypnosis is often referred to as Covert Hypnosis, even though there are some distinctions between the two.

Milton H. Erickson, M.D.

Milton Erickson is considered the father of modern hypnotherapy. The technique he created, Ericksonian hypnotherapy, is one of the fastest growing and influential branches of hypnotherapy today. His methods have inspired short term strategic therapy, the rebirth of guided imagery, and NLP. Even John Bradshaw, in both of his acclaimed series on PBS, frequently quotes Erickson and calls him "the greatest therapist who ever lived."

What sets Ericksonian Hypnosis apart from other, more traditional forms of **hypnosis**? Perhaps the best way to provide insight into this question is to follow Erickson's lead and use metaphors, starting with Erickson's own dramatic life story. It is a story of courage and determination that confirms my belief that everything happens for a reason.

Erickson was born in a rural farming country in 1902. The schooling he and many of his brothers and sisters received was basic, and thus it is not surprising that nobody noticed that young Milton was experiencing the world in a rather unique manner: he was color blind, tone deaf, and slightly dyslexic.

In the summer of 1919, at the age of seventeen, he was stricken with his first attack of Polio (his second would come at the age of fifty-one). It was an extremely severe infection, and he wasn't expected to survive. When he awoke from a coma three days later he found himself completely paralyzed, unable to move except for his eyes, and barely able to speak. Since there were no rehabilitation facilities in their community, there was no reason to expect that he'd ever recover.

Because all he had to entertain himself was his mind, Milton played mental games with himself. He learned to notice the difference between his family's verbal and non-verbal communications. He noticed that sometimes people would say "no" with their mouth while their body was clearly saying "yes." He also found that his body would occasionally respond when he imagined going outside (an indirect suggestion). It didn't respond when he commanded his body to move (a direct suggestion). By applying his discovery and watching his baby sister learning to walk, Milton taught himself to walk again.

Because of his experiences, he developed and pioneered the use of indirect suggestion, imagination, metaphor, and sensory acuity. He also influenced the following NLP presuppositions.

- Every behavior has a positive intention.

- People always make the best choice, based on what choices are available to them.

- Each individual operates from their own model of the world, and that model must be respected.

- There are no resistant clients, only inflexible therapists. Resistance is simply a lack of rapport.

Patients are patients because they're out of rapport with their own unconscious minds. This theory guided much of Erickson's work. He believed that when there was a rapport between the conscious and unconscious minds, then every intention of the mind would be carried out by the body. For example, if I want to lift a glass of water I can do so easily by just thinking about it. The muscles move perfectly, because I have clarity of purpose. However, if there is a break in this rapport, like a limiting belief or self sabotage, then I may fail to lift the glass. This is why we work with parts and shifting limiting beliefs with NLP. By removing obstacles to success, we create a rapport between our conscious and unconscious minds.

Often, Erickson didn't use a formal trace induction. Instead he told stories and metaphors that were layered with meaning. Sometimes that meaning was clear, but most times the person's conscious mind couldn't immediately grasp it. In these cases, Erickson aimed to illuminate the resources the client needed to solve their own problem. Eventually the meaning would become clear, and the client could utilize their learning by making a change.

The following fundamentals cover all the basics of Ericksonian Hypnotherapy. The first six aspects are considered covert techniques and will be explained in greater detail in this section. Fundamentals 6 and 7 will be explained further in subsequent chapters.

- Fundamental 1: Permissive Trance
- Fundamental 2: Embedded Commands
- Fundamental 3: Utilization
- Fundamental 4 : Negation
- Fundamental 5: Storytelling
- Fundamental 6: Time Distortion
- Fundamental 7: Ordeal Therapy

FUNDAMENTAL 1: PERMISSIVE TRANCE

As mentioned above, Erickson was well known for using indirect suggestion. He understood the importance of allowing, rather than forcing. Most other hypnotists at the time were using an authoritarian style, giving direct commands. This style, while still valid, is more likely to encounter resistance. Milton avoided resistance by telling stories and using permissive language, which gave the client the feeling of being in control. Nevertheless, Erickson's suggestions affected the client's outcome.

The permissive style of hypnosis is also more readily accepted by clients that are unsure about being hypnotized, clients that are polarity responders (individuals that always respond in reverse to a given command), and those that don't like following orders. You may be thinking this is everyone, and you could be right.

EXAMPLES OF PERMISSIVE LANGUAGE

- "You may decide to relax a little now."

- "If you could feel really wonderful, you'd likely recognize the value of trance."

- "While you browse the deals we have available, it might be a good idea to make your purchase quickly, so you can feel sure you got a great deal."

- Magic Words: may, might, could, can, want, it's possible, likely

FUNDAMENTAL 2: EMBEDDED COMMANDS

As mentioned above, Erickson used indirect, permissive language to get through conscious resistance, but within this indirect language he embedded direct suggestions. He would make the commands stand out from the larger sentence structure by varying his tonality, volume, or by gesturing at the appropriate time. This would signal the unconscious to pay special attention to the command.

To make my use of embedded commands obvious, throughout the rest of the book I have underlined each command I give examples for. You may recognize, by the end of the book, just how to <u>utilize embedded commands</u>.

USING EMBEDDED COMMANDS

- "You may listen to my voice, as it drifts in the air, and you might <u>feel relaxed</u>."

- "In a moment, you could <u>remember happy times</u>."

- "There are things that drift away, <u>like the sounds</u> of passing things."
- "You could, <u>like me</u>, get a great deal."

Fundamental 3: Utilization

When I had my first office in San Diego, the building's water pipes ran through the ceiling of the room where I did hypnosis. Inevitably I would have a client deep in trance, and someone on the other side of the building would flush a toilet. The sound of water rushing through the pipes would startle the clients awake, until I learned the process of **utilization**.

Utilization is the use of the current situation, whether it's resistance or something that could interrupt your results, to your benefit. So, as soon as I'd hear that water I would say, "And now you're flushing away all those old feelings, releasing them completely from your body and your life." The results were amazing! Clients would come out of trance excited that sounds could be so real in hypnosis!

Erickson employed utilization mostly in regards to resistance. If a client didn't feel comfortable enough to go into trance, or if they were resisting a particular suggestion he would use their resistance against them. An example of this is the **more-more pattern** Erickson often used. If a client didn't want to close their eyes, he would say, "The more you resist <u>closing your eyes now</u>, the heavier your eyelids become, and the deeper in trance you go."

Another benefit of utilization is that it takes advantage of the mind's penchant for linkages. The mind is literally a linking machine. Everything we have learned throughout our lives has been done through linking. There are two types of links; cause and effect links and complex equivalences. The first time you turned on a light switch, and the lights came on, you made a cause and effect link between light switches and light. Eventually this learning generalized to dimmer switches, knobs, and pulls. Cause and effect is an effective learning tool, because it generally is one-time learning. However, I consider complex equivalence learning faulty logic. A complex equivalence is a statement where you connect two things in such a way as to imply that if the first thing is true then the other must be true as well. For example, if the lights go on when I flip the switch, I could take it to mean that the gods, because of my goodness, have granted me with light. This link isn't necessarily correct, but our tendency to make these types of associations means we can use them to create trance and generate influence.

UTILIZING UTILIZATION

- "As you feel the trembling on the floor and hear the rattling of the shelves, <u>break down old walls</u> of limitation."

- "Because you've invested a lot of time and money in your search for a great house, [that means] you deserve the best, and it appears <u>you've found it here</u>."

- "During your physical relaxation <u>you learned to do hypnosis</u>, and once you learn how to do something you can <u>do it even better</u> now."

- "While you <u>consider all the possibilities</u> that utilization has to offer, you'll recognize your misconceptions, and <u>begin creating</u> new and more useful ones now."

- Magic Words: as, while, during, because, that means, consequently

FUNDAMENTAL 4: NEGATION

Erickson, of course, used language and suggestion to induce a hypnotic state and make changes. And in this context, he found the use of negation to be useful in bypassing conscious resistance. However, this type of resistance also occurs in the sales environment. Therefore, negative suggestions can be useful in both situations.

Negation is the use of suggestions that instruct a listener on what not to do. If I told you not to take something personally, you're more likely to do so. This is due to the fact that the unconscious mind can't create a negative image, or the image of not doing something. And if I were to say to you, "I'm not considering you <u>remember feeling good</u>," you're likely to do just that.

By giving negative suggestions, you're able to be covert, using indirect suggestion. This means you're bypassing the critical factor, or satisfying the conscious objection, while commanding the unconscious to act.

Using Negation

- "People can sleep and not know they're asleep. They can dream and not remember the dream. You don't know when <u>the eyelids will close</u> all by themselves."

- "I'm not telling you not to <u>care deeply for yourself</u> in ways you <u>do it now</u>."

- "It's important that you don't make this purchase any sooner than you feel comfortable doing so."

- "Whatever you do, don't <u>buy now</u> and you'll recognize the importance of <u>feeling sure</u> you're making the right decision."

- Magic Words: not, don't, can't, won't, wouldn't, couldn't

Fundamental 5: Storytelling

Probably the most notable element of Ericksonian Hypnosis, storytelling is what really set Erickson apart from his contemporaries. Storytelling builds on the concept of indirect suggestion, and aids a client in finding a solution to a particular problem by accessing resources in another context. The mind can then connect those resources to the applicable context.

I had a client recently that had a hard time forgiving her father for withdrawing his affection. She had been told directly by many practitioners and friends that she needed to forgive him, but she just couldn't. Every time she would think of him, she'd start getting really upset. I asked her if she ever withheld sweets or junk food from her young boys, and she confirmed she did. When I asked why, she replied she didn't think those foods were good for them. I then proceeded to ask if any other parents she knew did things differently, and when she confirmed this as well, I knew I had a good angle. So, I casually mentioned that parents all have differing views on what is healthy, and what kids should have and not have. And they all still love their children. She understood and forgave her father.

Milton's teaching tales ranged from deeply complex to relatively simple. They all had a definite structure, although some were largely metaphorical, while others were more straightforward.

FUNDAMENTAL 6: TIME DISTORTION

One of the effects of hypnosis is time distortion, the experience of time going faster or slower than normal. Because time is subjective in the hypnotic state, the techniques of regression and progression are easily utilized. Milton Erickson often used regression to disconnect unpleasant emotions from specific memories and to access resources from the past. While Erickson wasn't the only hypnotist doing regression, he pioneered the use of dissociation to relieve the client's suffering. Other popular hypnotherapists, like Dave Elman, conducted regression with full association, guiding the client to relive the painful experience so as to create an abreaction, or emotional release. Erickson believed that strong emotion is helpful in the therapeutic process, but he instead utilized positive resource emotions to create change.

The use of progression was pioneered by Erickson. He agreed with psychologist, Alfred Adler, that individuals are more motivated by the future than by the past. This led Erickson to build what Bandler and Grinder came to call "a compelling future" for his clients. By infusing the future with intense, pleasurable emotions and vivid imagery, clients could imagine their lives taking a different trajectory than the one they had previously created for themselves.

Progression is one of the most important tools available to NLP practitioners, and you'll find it in nearly every published process, because it creates generative change. It isn't enough to change how you feel about the past. If you don't create a future that is also different, you'll continue to relive the past. In order for changes you make with clients to stick and really work, you need to future pace the change.

FUNDAMENTAL 7: ORDEAL THERAPY

Erickson is famous for pioneering indirect techniques, but his shock therapy shows that he was prepared to use psychological shocks and ordeals in order to achieve results. Erickson's use of ordeals inspired the NLP presupposition that if something doesn't work, try something else. Erickson truly embodied the idea of behavioral flexibility, doing whatever was necessary to assist the client.

There are a large number of examples of Erickson's approaches to ordeal therapy. In one instance, he urged a married couple to intentionally wet the bed in order to stop doing so unintentionally. In another example, Erickson encouraged a young woman to seduce a man in an elevator to reduce his fear of riding in elevators. Once he even attempted to hypnotize a man in the midst of a psychotic episode. It took over 12 hours, but Milton just kept at it. In these circumstances, Erickson was using shock to break their normal pattern, or strategy. We now call this technique a **pattern interrupt**.

Using shock, and being willing to do what it takes to help a client achieve their results, is at the heart of the practice of NLP. In order to be effective, you have to think creatively and try new techniques, even if they seem silly or extreme (but not dangerous, of course).

CHAPTER 19:
THE MILTON MODEL

In the 1970s Gregory Bateson was enthusiastic about the Meta Model approach of getting more specific and precise about problems, because it gave clients new resources and solutions to problems. He was also aware of the work of Milton Erickson, who was getting great results with his clients by being vague rather than specific. Bateson encouraged John Grinder and Richard Bandler to meet Erickson and discover why he was so successful. Their description of Erickson's language patterns became known as the Milton Model.

"The Milton Model is a way of using language to induce and maintain trance in order to contact hidden resources of our personality. It follows the way the mind works naturally. Trance is a state where you are highly motivated to learn from your unconscious mind in an inner directed way. It is not a passive state, nor are you under another's influence. There is co-operation between client and therapist, the client's responses letting the therapist know what to do next." Joseph O'Connor

The Milton Model is grouped in three categories; Presuppositions, Indirect Elicitation Patterns, and Patterns in Metaphor. While those words may sound big and scary, the patterns themselves are fairly simple.

PRESUPPOSITIONS

Presuppositions are assumptions made in advance. Milton would often ask someone, "Do you want to go into trance in this chair or that one?" This would presuppose the client would go into trance and it would happen in one of those chairs, which is a covert way of creating a resourceful belief. Another example would be, "When would you like to schedule your next appointment?"

Presuppositions come in a variety of ways; time, order, choice, consciousness, adverbs and adjectives.

Milton was known for distorting time, such as suggesting, "Would you like to use the restroom before you go into trance?" Another option here is, "Do you prefer me to explain the options while you're making your purchase, or would you like me to wait until the purchase is complete?"

Another type of presupposition regards the order in which things are done. I can imagine Milton saying, "It's possible that you could go into trance first." This presupposes that there are subsequent things that will happen, or that trance could happen at another time. I'm fond of using, "The third insight you have today..." The best part about using this pattern is that the other steps don't even need to be specified.

Probably the most commonly used presupposition is choice. Erickson often used options to give the illusion that the client had free will, which they did, but his language usually resulted in the response he expected. For example, "Would you prefer relaxing with your feet up or with your back straight?" I've been known to use, "Would you like to pay for this in full, or would you prefer to make payment arrangements?" Either way, they are paying!

Consciousness predicates are words that indicate awareness. Because Ericksonian Hypnosis is based on downtime trance, or trance that is inwardly focused (as opposed to uptime trance, which is outwardly focused), using words that draw an individual's attention inward will create a deeper state of hypnosis. For example, "Are you aware of how your breath moves in and out?" This statement presupposes that the breathing was already there, it was only a matter of becoming aware of it. Or, "Do you recognize how good you feel, now that you've made the decision to take home this car today?"

There are a few different types of adverbs and adjectives that Erickson would use. Some were used to enhance an experience, as in "How easily can you go into trance?" Others focused on changing time, such as, "Feel free to continue shopping." Milton would also use commentary, lending judgment to his statements, as in, "Luckily, you're being hypnotized by a professional." These words can also be used to presuppose that whatever is going on is fortunate. For example, "Thankfully, we have just one item left in stock."

Now, I should mention that Ericksonian language can sound confusing, mostly because it is. Confusion is an excellent technique for creating trance, and the purpose of using this language is not to be grammatically correct but to influence behavior in a positive way. With that said, there are some contexts that lend themselves well to only certain patterns. You wouldn't necessarily use the patterns in exactly the same way in sales as you would to create a hypnotic state, or at least not yet. Here is an example of stringing together a series of presuppositions within the hypnosis context.

Would you prefer to tell me your problem first, or would you rather just <u>go deeply in trance</u>, since you can find all the resources necessary on your first try. And you may become aware, as you think of things to tell me about your problem, of the rise and fall of your chest, the images in your mind, and they may already be changing while you continue to <u>comfortably relax</u>. And I don't know just how quickly your solution will appear, as you notice your eyes growing heavy and very relaxed.

Would you like to go through all the tedious contract details first, or would you rather just test drive some great cars, since <u>buy now</u> you already know how exciting it is to smell that new smell and notice the feel of the insides. You don't need another person making fun of your old car. It's time for change, and luckily you came here on the perfect day to end your search.

MAGIC WORDS

Time: before, after, during, as, since, prior, when, while, begin, end, stop, start, continue, proceed, already, yet, still, anymore, etc.

Order: another, first, second, third, etc.

Choice: or

Consciousness: aware, notice, recognize, know, understand, etc.

Adverbs and Adjectives: luckily, realistically, happily, easily, deeply, curious about, etc.

INDIRECT ELICITATION PATTERNS

The following patterns involve the tone of voice as much as the words themselves. Erickson was a master of tonality, using just the right inflection to get the response he was after. In order to master the following patterns, practice adjusting the way in which you use the words. Fairly quickly you will notice how to generate maximum impact.

- Embedded Commands
- Embedded Questions
- Negative Commands
- Conversational Postulates
- Ambiguity

A notable element of Ericksonian Hypnosis is the use of **Embedded Commands**. These are hypnotic suggestions that indicate a response, regardless of the rest of the sentence it is embedded within. As mentioned previously, embedded commands should be marked out with a slight shift in tonality, volume, or gestures. But be sure to do so discreetly. If embedded commands are marked out too obviously, your suggestion could backfire and break rapport. For clarity, these commands are underlined. Can you discover embedded commands? Or, maybe you'd prefer to understand completely.

Embedded Questions sound like statements, but they are really asking a question. They will often be answered as if they had been asked directly. One example is, "I'm wondering what time it is." This sentence indicates that the speaker wants the listener to tell him the time, without overtly saying so. This pattern is particularly useful for resistant individuals, because it gives them the opportunity to cooperate without knowing they are doing so. And again, this is based on tonality. Embedded questions should sound like statements, rather than questions, in which the tone of voice goes up at the end. Right? Instead, the tone of a command should be relatively flat to indicate a general statement. Another example of an embedded question is, "I'm curious to know how you will use this vehicle."

Negative Commands are fundamental to Ericksonian Hypnosis. Because whatever you do, don't <u>learn the Milton Model</u>. As you read previously, the word "don't" is not processed by the unconscious mind in the same way as it is in the conscious mind. The unconscious ignores the not and creates an image of whatever you're suggesting. So, don't <u>purchase that car</u> yet. Let the good feelings really sink in first.

Conversational Postulates are yes/no questions that typically elicit a response rather than a literal answer. By using them you'll get a response without directly asking for it. For example, "Are you aware of what's happening in there?" Or, "Are you going to finish that?" Beginning to understand?

One of the most interesting and fun categories of the Milton Model is *Ambiguity*, which is comprised of four distinctions; phonological, syntactic, scope, and punctuation. Sometimes things can be interpreted two or more ways. When a meaning is unclear, it's ambiguous. Most communicators believe ambiguity is best avoided, but that's because they don't know how to use it properly. What they don't realize is that the unconscious mind processes every possible meaning of a communication.

Understanding ambiguity is also useful to ensure that you don't inadvertently convey an unintended meaning. I read a headline a few years ago that said, "Prostitutes Appeal to Pope." Now, I'm sure the author meant to say that prostitutes were making an appeal to the pope regarding an issue, but it could also come across as the pope was finding the prostitutes appealing. Oops!

Ambiguities also take up a lot of brain power for the listener to process. When the conscious mind gets overloaded trying to figure out the meanings, the unconscious mind becomes more open to suggestion. This is confusion, which you understand creates a deeper state of hypnosis. The use of **Ambiguity** also requires the listener to actively participate in the communication, because it requires making connections and sorting meaning.

Phonological Ambiguities are words that sound alike but have different meanings. For example, the word *right* sounds like *write* and *rite*. So, the phrase, "You may want to make the right passage," could be interpreted differently, depending on the listener. If I was hypnotizing a writer, passage means something different than it does to a sailor. Phonological Ambiguities can take the form of nouns or verbs. Here are a few examples to get you started.

- Nouns: I/eye, right/write/rite, weight/wait, their/they're/there, red/read, by/buy

- Verbs: Push, pull, rest, nod, talk, touch, point, hand, feel

Syntactic Ambiguities occur when the function of a word is unclear. There are two forms of this type of ambiguity that Erickson used; verb + ing + noun and nominalization of nouns. The first type is probably the easiest to use. An example is, "They were walking dogs." In that statement, it is unclear whether they are dogs that are walking, or if they are people that are taking dogs for a walk. An example of the second form is, "You may understand the feeling of a rolling stone." It is unclear whether they are meant to feel the texture of a stone, or if they are meant to understand how a rolling stone feels emotionally.

- Inspiring decorators can be fun.

- Do you enjoy exciting people?

- The touch of the sun/son can be enlightening.

- I wonder if you could buy the books on the counter.

- You're a bigger man than me.

Scope Ambiguities occur when it is unclear how much of the sentence an adjective, verb, or adverb applies to. Erickson may have said, "I wonder if you could cut the grass with my sister." It is unclear whether you are meant to assist my sister in cutting the grass, or if you are meant to use my sister as a lawnmower.

- They went with the charming men and women.

- I don't know how fully you will realize that you are going deeply into trance and feeling good.

- I am speaking to you as a child.

Punctuation Ambiguities are two distinct sentences strung together by using the last word of one sentence as the first word of the second. For example, "I really like your tie into that thought." Using this type of ambiguity is very effective in influencing behavior, even though it requires a little more practice than the other types of ambiguities.

- I'm speaking clearly to make sure you can hear/here <u>you are feeling good</u>.
- Many hands make light work smarter.
- Are you going to walk buy the videos are on sale today.

Here's one way to generate a scope ambiguity...

1. Pick a goal, like inducing trance.
2. Create a sentence with a subject acting on a thing or a person and that includes the goal ("She slipped into trance.").
3. Add a descriptive term to the person or thing being acted upon ("She gently slipped into deep trance.").
4. List something or several things in such a way as to be unclear whether or not the earlier part of the sentence applies to the later parts ("She gently slipped into deep trance, breathed, and remembered feeling good.").

I would recommend making a list of a variety of ambiguities, separated by type, which you can use in your work. Then, you can practice delivering them to your clients and co-workers to see how well they work.

PATTERNS IN METAPHOR

The two following patterns are particularly useful when doing hypnosis or when using metaphors in communication. Neither pattern exists in the Meta Model; they are additional patterns in the Milton Model.

The first pattern is known as a **Selectional Restriction Violation** (SRV), or the attribution of qualities to something that can not actually possess those qualities. Two examples of this are attributing feelings to inanimate objects ("The nail hurt my tire.") and associating a particular predicate with an inappropriate object ("The car inhaled deeply.").

The purpose of an SRV is to generate a search for meaning. Milton would even encourage the search by adding the client's name ("The nail, John, hurt my tire.") or by pointing out that the statement was odd ("It's strange to consider a car inhaling deeply, isn't it?").Because it is an unusual way to speak, the listener is forced to create meaning. This causes the listener to turn their attention inward, often leading them to apply the statement to themselves.

The final Milton Model pattern is **Quotes**, which is a covert way to deliver a message. I used to work for a nonprofit agency, and one day I had a bad experience with a volatile client. I was left in the building alone, and he threatened me with a weapon. It was against policy to leave anyone alone, and I wanted to express this delicately and without blame. So, I told my boss at the time, "I was talking with a friend yesterday, because he had been arguing with his girlfriend who had said, 'I can't believe you left me alone. Something very bad could have happened to me, and then you would have had to live with the guilt of it forever.' I suggested he ask for an apology and a promise never to do that again." In that way, I was able to deliver my message indirectly, saving him from embarrassment, and me from an unpleasant confrontation.

Another way to use quotes is in the development of trance ("Yesterday a client came to see me, and I told him to relax very deeply, listening to my voice, and resting comfortably."). I find it particularly helpful when teaching a client a lesson they aren't ready to consciously accept ("Milton once said to his client, you can't change without letting your preconceptions go now.")

Inverting the Meta Model

The patterns listed above are unique to the Milton Model, and so are grouped separately. But the Milton Model is also the reverse of the Meta Model. The following patterns are the Meta Model distinctions, except instead of using them to get more specific in your communication, you will use them to become artfully vague. When doing hypnosis, it's far more useful to use vague language, because it prompts the listener to fill in the blanks. This engages more of the imagination, which is helpful in trance formation.

Gathering Information (Deletions)

In these patterns, all specific information is deleted. I find this chunk of the Milton Model to be the most useful for inducing hypnosis, because it forces the listener to fill in the blanks with their imagination. The following four patterns are forms of deletions.

- Nominalizations

- Unspecified Predicates
- Lack of Referential Index
- Comparative Deletions

Nominalizations are process words, or verbs, that have been frozen in time by turning them into nouns. For example, the word "relationship" is a nominalization, because it really describes the process of relating. In the Meta Model, we challenged nominalizations, but when doing hypnosis it's best to use them to your advantage. The purpose of nominalizations is to empower the listener to draw their own conclusion, rather than giving direct suggestion.

I am aware that you were experiencing *difficulties* and that you now understand how to utilize the learnings you have to develop the *resources* required to reach your perfect solution. This moment can provide you with *new insights* and *new clarity* to make this change now.

I know that you have been *experiencing trouble* with this *issue*, and you would like it to come to *resolution*. I don't know whether your *mind* will handle it effectively, or if you will have a *new experience*, or just let it go.

Unspecified Predicates / Unspecified Verbs aid in the induction of hypnosis as well. Keep in mind, the more unspecified you are, the more the listener has to fill in the blanks. This creates a very unique experience for the listener, and the coach or hypnotist rarely knows what that experience is.

And you understand how to just *let go*, and relax fully and completely. Notice how easily you begin to *think* good thoughts, because you can experience *going* there.

Magic Words: do, fix, solve, move, change, wonder, think, sense, know, experience, understand, remember, become aware of, etc.

Lack of Referential Index is a phrase that doesn't pick out a specific portion of the listener's experience. Or, the noun has been left out or unspecified.

One can, you know, learn the Milton Model easily. *Some individuals* find it useful to absorb new information.

Magic Words: some, one, people, particular, this, it, individual, specific, they, etc.

Comparative Deletions / Unspecified Comparisons are phrases where a comparison is made, although to whom or to what it is made is not specified. Using this pattern gives the illusion of a comparison, and can enhance a suggestion.

It is *more or less* the right thing, because *now and then* things happen that let you know you can be *even more* relaxed and curious, because at *one time or another* you may get it done.

SEMANTIC ILL-FORMEDNESS (DISTORTION)

Distortion is a process by which we create either limitations or resources by inaccurately representing something in our neurology or language. Distortion often occurs when we use language to describe, generalize, and theorize about our experience. Using distortion gives you the opportunity to create the experience that is most helpful for the listener. These patterns will assist you in guiding the communication in the most useful direction.

I recommend these patterns for working in therapeutic settings, in customer service, and in advertising.

Cause and Effect links imply one thing causes another. I like to think of this as if/then statements. Use this pattern to link anything that is true to something that you want to have happen. For example, if you want someone to sign a contract, suggest that because they fell in love with the house they will sign. Or, if you need to pacify an angry customer, you can suggest that because they got you on the phone, their issue will be resolved.

As you read this text, you are beginning to understand fully how this language is beneficial to you. Don't keep reading, *unless* you want to go into trance.

Magic Words: because, as, unless, (use with negation), while if/then, more

Complex Equivalences occur when the meanings of two separate things are equated, or have equivalent meaning. To use this pattern, suggest that a behavior or situation has a particular meaning. This can be used to direct the situation in a positive way.

Reading this text *means* that you are learning many things.

You've viewed several housing options, and the fact that you finally found one you absolutely love *means* you're ready for the next step, *so* feel free to take a moment to read the contract to ensure <u>it meets your approval</u>.

Magic Words: that means, so, suggests, indicates

Mind Reading is claiming to know the thoughts or feelings of another without specifying the process by which you came to know the information. This pattern builds the credibility of the speaker, as long as it is done correctly, by using vague language.

I know that you are wondering how <u>you will learn this</u>. And, you are *probably aware* of reading this now, so you can take it in and <u>process it effectively</u>.

You may be curious about the products we have available, and how you <u>can purchase them now</u>.

A **Lost Performative** is a value judgment where the person making the evaluation is left out. Statements using this pattern can be an effective way of delivering presuppositions. Think of this as the "says who?" pattern from the Meta Model. The value of this pattern, to me, is that it lends credence to what you want the listener to do. It creates value and attaches it to the desired behavior.

It's a good thing to wonder how easily <u>you will learn this</u>.

When searching for the right car, *it's important* to evaluate the options and follow your intuition. You will know if <u>this is the right car for you</u>.

Magic Words: that's right, it's important, it's good, it's helpful, etc.

LIMITS OF THE SPEAKER'S MODEL (GENERALIZATION)

Generalization occurs when you draw global conclusions about yourself or the world around you based on one or two experiences. At its best, generalization is one of the ways that we learn, by taking the information we have and drawing broad conclusions about the meaning of the effect of those conclusions. If used improperly it can cause trouble by making a problem seem larger than it actually is. But, for our purposes here, generalizations aid in trance induction.

Universal Quantifiers are a set of words that have both universal generalization and a lack of referential index. I like to think of these words as gross generalizations, and they are useful in the hypnotic environment, because they affect internal representations.

Every meaning will be clear as you breathe and relax. *All* the understanding will come in time, and you can <u>now fully understand</u> the Milton Model. *Each* of the things you don't yet comprehend <u>become clear</u> at just the right moment.

Magic Words: all, every, always, never, nobody, no one, each, none

Modal Operators are words that imply necessity or form rules. There are modal operators of necessity and possibility. These words influence behavior by either granting permission or restricting choice.

You *must* be getting this now at some level. You *may* be able to <u>use this effectively</u> now and then, because you *should* feel free to <u>practice</u> using modal operators.

Magic Words for Necessity: should, must, have to, can't, won't

Magic Words for Possibility: can, may, might, could

PUTTING IT ALL TOGETHER NOW...

As you sit there, reading these words, feeling the chair beneath you, you are probably aware of your breathing, and that means <u>you are relaxing now</u>. I know that you are wondering, and it's a good thing to wonder how deeply <u>you can go into trance</u>. And all things, all things that you used to think about hypnosis are being replaced by this experience, now you are past the point of where <u>learning takes place hear</u> my words and <u>go deeper</u> into <u>you're unconscious</u> where you can do this even better, and now you must be getting this at some level, because hypnosis is easy. And as you <u>let go</u>, you can, you know, <u>feel good</u>, can you not? Now and then things happen to help you <u>feel relaxed and comfortable</u>, and as you breathe and blink, you can <u>begin now</u> or later, to <u>go into a trance</u> experience is similar to what Richard told me about <u>hypnosis inside your mind</u> it is really simple since even a chair can relax. Can you imagine doing this now? You can, you know, <u>do it well</u>.

CHAPTER 20:
THERAPEUTIC METAPHORS

A metaphor is a representation of an object or an idea with which it shares a similar quality. A metaphor is deeply embedded in our language, culture, and the way we think. Therefore, it affects how we interact with the world and other people.

A symbol is the smallest unit of metaphor, consisting of a single object, image, or word representing the essence of the quality or attribute for which it stands. For example, a candle flame may be a symbolic representation of the Divine Light within an individual, while a coin may be a symbolic representation of abundance.

Archetypes serve as metaphors for how to live, behave, and feel. The lover archetype, for example, acts as a representation of living with your heart open, while the warrior archetype serves to guide setting and enforcing boundaries.

Every individual experiences the world in metaphorical terms. How many times have you heard "It's raining cats and dogs," or "I'm going out on a limb here?" Metaphors describe our experiences in a way that conveys their true meaning, both to ourselves and to others. Nearly every teacher, spiritual and otherwise, uses metaphors to make complex concepts understandable, because they have the ability to take understanding from one context and apply it to another. For example, you already understand that you create your experience of life, and to explain how that is I might tell you a story about going into your closet and trying on everything you own to decide what to keep and what to let go. Got it?

Metaphors can be used in any situation and in nearly every communication, from therapy to sales. You've been using them your whole life. Now, you'll understand how to use them more consciously and effectively.

STEPS TO BUILDING A THERAPEUTIC METAPHOR

Metaphors are more than a way to talk about an experience. They are experience. They set the filters through which we perceive and make sense out of the world. Because of this fact, metaphors serve as powerful levers, capable of shifting perception and experience. And, as a result, you can transform people's behavior by developing a resourceful metaphor.

Milton Erickson was renowned for his ability to assist people in making dramatic personal change, and for people who didn't recognize what he was doing, Erickson simply told stories, parables, or jokes. However, others like Bandler and Grinder recognized there were deeper patterns at work.

Erickson told stories to bypass conscious resistance to change. It's very difficult to guard yourself against a lesson that is told about someone else. Most of us listen intently to stories, and we immerse ourselves in their imagery in order to fully understand their meaning. And because our unconscious minds take everything personally, we begin to apply the stories to our own experiences, filling in the gaps with our own experiences. Well told, inspiring stories will affect us personally. Consider the book, *The Alchemist*, by Paolo Coelho, which has inspired millions around the globe to turn the lead in their lives into gold.

Telling a therapeutic metaphor is very similar to planting seeds. Some spring forth immediately while others sprout sometime in the future. The real beauty of a metaphor is the ability to affect deep and lasting change in an indirect and covert manner.

In his landmark book, Therapeutic Metaphors, David Gordon explains, in depth, how to build an excellent metaphor. It is a must-read for anyone seeking to master the art of storytelling. But, for our purposes here, I have distilled the critical elements to creating a powerful and therapeutic story.

SET A WELL FORMED OUTCOME.

Without a specific outcome, it is difficult to develop an appropriate metaphor that will address all of the client's concerns. For example, a couple experiencing marital trouble due to an interloping mother-in-law might set the outcome of keeping her in their lives, but being able to set and enforce reasonable boundaries for her, without resentment.

THE METAPHOR MUST BE EQUIVALENT TO THE CIRCUMSTANCES SURROUNDING THE CLIENT'S PROBLEM.

In other words, the relationships and events should closely resemble those of the present state without being exactly the same. For example, the previously noted couple experiencing marital trouble might become two rabbits being annoyed by ants at their picnic.

THE METAPHOR MUST OFFER AN APPROPRIATE RESOLUTION.

The purpose of telling a therapeutic metaphor is to assist the client in finding an appropriate solution to their problem. It may be the one you present in your tale, but it may be another option your metaphor helped unlock. To continue from the example above, the resolution may be to direct the ants to someone or something else more deserving of their attention, like something sweet.

A THERAPEUTIC METAPHOR CHANGES THE PROBLEM STRATEGY, AND PROVIDES A CONNECTION TO A RESOURCEFUL BEHAVIOR OR FEELING.

Every problem has a strategy, which becomes evident in information gathering. A successful metaphor deletes the strategy and provides a way for the client to change themselves and, thereby, the situation. Still working with the example above, it would be safe to imply that the rabbits began to notice the important work that ants do, and because they make waste disappear, that understanding can help the couple to change how they feel. The new strategy could also include leading the ants to something they like more than the rabbit's picnic.

THE MAIN OBJECTIVE OF A THERAPEUTIC METAPHOR IS REFRAMING.

Reframing is the act of changing a limiting belief or behavior into a resource. Therefore, the ants aren't interlopers; they are vital parts to the forest ecosystem. They get rid of the things you don't want anymore. Another reframe that could be useful relates to the couple's interaction with each other. While they are bickering amongst themselves, the ants are taking over. If they need to talk about the situation, its best that they work together to enjoy their picnic.

THERAPEUTIC METAPHORS HAVE A SPECIFIC SYNTAX THAT MAKES THEM EFFECTIVE.

First, metaphors employ a lack of referential index. If a noun doesn't have to be specified in order for the story to make sense, it's best to leave it unspecified. Instead of suggesting that sugar water be used to lure the ants back home, consider using sweetness to lead them in a positive direction. Second, use nominalizations liberally. While challenging nominalizations is helpful for gathering information, metaphors work best when they are vague. Instead of suggesting the rabbits devise a three-step plan to rid the picnic of ants, consider saying, "And they turned to each other, bound by their mutual objective, to form a united front." Metaphors also use embedded commands and analog marking. Because the telling of metaphors is considered conversational hypnosis, using hypnotic language and embedded commands is key to making a positive change.

EFFECTIVE METAPHORS ALSO USE REPRESENTATIONAL SYSTEMS AND SUBMODALITIES.

As with any good story, providing sensory information keeps the listener engaged and the imagination active. Additionally, representational systems can also assist the listener in finding an appropriate solution. By speaking in the listener's preferred system, in regards to the presenting issue, you're more likely to convey your meaning.

You already understand the importance of making submodality shifts, and you can also do them with metaphors. By transforming the interloping mother in law into an ant, you've changed the size of the internal image. Additionally, if we had gathered that the way in which the mother in law irritated the couple was by calling frequently to get herself invited to every family event, and that the couple's experience of this was the abrasive sound of her voice, followed by an extremely large, looming picture the change would become obvious. By making the internal image smaller and lower in the visual field, the couple's experience would be different.

Ericksonian Metaphors

Erickson's method for creating therapeutic metaphors and stories is very detailed. However, using the concepts you have already learned, you will be able to easily construct a therapeutic metaphor by meeting these additional criteria.

Use the Milton Model.

Unspecified words allow the listener to fill in the details for themselves. Milton was well known for being "artfully vague." This ensured that the listener could apply the story to their own life experience, and it prompted the listener to fill in the blanks with their own understandings. *There are lots of learnings and understandings that you have had in the past that you have consciously forgotten about before now. You can go to a certain time and certain place to get what you need.*

Use modal operators of possibility and permission to empower the listener. Operators of necessity are often interpreted as preaching, to which many individuals have resistance. By using permissive language, the listener receives the suggestions in a softer form, making it more likely they will be receptive. *Feel free to take only what is useful here. You can experience whatever you choose to at this time.*

Effective therapeutic metaphors use subject and object deletion. The listener is already aware of the issue, so stating it specifically isn't necessary; it may actually backfire and cause resistance. *Guidance can be received in many ways. Inside are all the resources you could ever need.*

Use a passive voice. Using too much detail about the process in which something happened can be detrimental. By omitting the "how" you allow the listener's unconscious mind to apply it's own direction. *Much was revealed in many, interesting and mysterious ways. Change can occur at any time.*

By using quotes and selectional restriction violations, you can give even more embedded and indirect suggestions, which is one of the main objectives in telling therapeutic metaphors.

Now, while Ericksonian metaphors leave much to the imagination, it is important to give enough detail and structure so that the story makes sense. Of course, that doesn't require much detail to do successfully. Here is a story I told a client recently.

You know, life can be very interesting. Just when you think you've got it all figured out, things happen, and you find yourself in a new place, feeling different and looking for some way to understand completely that which you've forgotten you already knew. And, when you think about it, you might gain clarity in new and more powerful ways, because you can see clearly that change can occur.

USE ANCHORING.

You can utilize auditory anchoring in metaphors to break unpleasant connections and establish new, more resourceful feelings. Set the anchors while the listener is in the state you want, then fire them off at the appropriate place in your story. It's an elegant and effective way to use anchoring.

CLASS OF PROBLEMS V. CLASS OF SOLUTIONS

According to Bill O'Hanlon, Milton Erickson structured most of his stories in a concrete way. Instead of just identifying the present and desired state for a client, he would break those down into types. For example, in one of his most famous stories about a ten year old boy with a bedwetting problem, he chunked down bedwetting into the following **class of problems**; lack of muscle control, poor timing, and lack of coordination. It's easy to assume that Erickson determined the following to be an appropriate **class of solutions**; muscle control, appropriate timing, and coordination. And in this case, Erickson told stories about baseball and archery, two of the boy's favorite sports. And because they both required coordination and timing, he was able to weave in several embedded commands for muscle control.

I have found the class of solutions approach very helpful in designing metaphors. By identifying the type of solution required, it is much easier to uncover an appropriate story. For clients dealing with public speaking fears, I find the most useful solutions are confidence and courage. Therefore, the story of the little engine that could often weaves its way in.

TELLING A THERAPEUTIC METAPHOR

Now, we all tell stories every day. But what defines a therapeutic metaphor? Some people believe a therapeutic story is a fairy tale or parable, and they are right. Those types of stories have messages and clear lessons. However, a well told anecdote can also be therapeutic. Drawing on personal experiences or telling about how others have overcome similar challenges is also a valuable approach. Just think about all the celebrities that have overcome problems, and the inspirational effect they have on the public.

Personally, when I tell a therapeutic metaphor, I rely on my own unconscious mind. I've had lots of experiences, both of my own and with clients. I have a storehouse of anecdotes from working with clients and students, but I also write some fairy tales and parables. This way, when I have a particular client in trance, and I've developed rapport, I allow my unconscious mind to present me with the appropriate story to tell. Occasionally I make one up on the spot. However you choose to do this is fine, yet I do recommend writing several before trying this out. It will ensure that you have the language correct, with the appropriate pauses and embedded commands.

Effective metaphors are told by great storytellers. If you plan to use them in your work, I would suggest studying Richard Bandler, Garrison Keillor, and Donald Davis in addition to Milton Erickson. They all *use rhythm and inflection* to make an impact on their listeners, and they are all skilled at using their voices to draw people into their stories. Keep in mind that tonality is important when telling stories!

"The logic of the emotional mind is associative; it takes elements that symbolize a reality, or trigger a memory of it, to be the same as that reality. That is why similes, metaphors and images speak directly to the emotional mind. If the emotional mind follows this logic and its rules, with one element standing for another, things need not necessarily be defined by their objective identity: what matters is how they are perceived; things are as they seem. Indeed, in emotional life, identities can be like a hologram in

the sense that a single part evokes a whole." Daniel Goleman, Emotional Intelligence

WHEN TO USE A METAPHOR

Although a story can be a useful addition to any session, they are best utilized when a client is living out an un-resourceful metaphor of their own design. People often tell us their metaphors, and sometimes all they need is a new one. For example:

> *I just feel like I'm coming apart at the seams.*
> *I'm stuck between a rock and a hard place.*
> *Life is an upward battle.*

So, in these cases, a therapeutic metaphor of another possible solution can be really helpful. Some examples to counter the above are:

> *Now, sometimes you can remember what it feels like to mend in new ways.*
> *What would it be like if you had the right tools to dig yourself out?*
> *Row, row, row your boat, gently down the stream...*

As you can see, a metaphor can be used to reframe a client's experience into something more positive and resourceful. And, as always, it is best to be framed in a way that they are helping themselves, rather than being helped by someone else.

Another opportunity to use a metaphor is when the client is stuck or resistant to change. Metaphors speak to another part of the mind, engaging the imagination and the feelings of possibility. They can help a client move into a more optimistic and positive space all on their own, which is both effective and empowering.

METAPHORS FOR BUSINESS AND SALES

Telling therapeutic metaphors is often different than using metaphor in business. For instance, in business, you'd want to stick to using anecdotes, rather than fairy tales and parables. Those types of metaphors can be too obtuse and lengthy to hold a customer's attention. However, telling anecdotes of other customers that have appreciated your product or service can go a long way. Often these are cited as testimonials, and they are very effective marketing tools.

Another way to use metaphors in business is in advertising. Many TV commercials employ metaphors. One great example is an Arby's Cherry Pie commercial. A beautiful woman hands an average looking guy her phone number, but his burger is so greasy that he accidentally smudges her number. Then, a sandwich that's "less greasy" is introduced. The intent is to anchor bad feelings to the greasy burger and attach good feelings to the new sandwich, which is done through a very simple story and memorable music.

Metaphors in business are short and to the point. They usually rely more on visualization to evoke states, and when used to close sales, they make use of embedded commands to purchase the product or service.

Other types of business metaphors are used in negotiation. These are often related to sports, war, and mental games. Not all are positive or foster the type of working environment that creates equality or good vibes. Here are a few I would suggest.

- "mending fences"
- "building bridges"
- "hammering out our differences"
- "working through our problem"

Metaphors are also used in organizations to indicate how the company is run. And again, some of them aren't totally positive or empowering. Some common metaphors are based around ships, as in running a tight ship or getting everyone on board. This can backfire, as there can only be one captain. A more empowering metaphor is that of a living organism, where every change effects the whole system. But use whatever is appropriate.

Essentially, building a business-related metaphor is a simple process. First, identify the resistance. What is your customer, employee, or client not doing that would be good for them? Then, identify something they enjoy or understand. This could be a sport like hiking or skydiving, or it could be something more sedentary like reading or talking with friends. Then, ask yourself how you can use that context as a metaphor or analogy to persuade them to overcome their resistance.

I had a student once that was planning to go into private practice as a hypnotherapist. However, she was resistant to becoming certified as a master practitioner of NLP. I found out she was a fast driver, so I used the following metaphor. "Think about the training this way. What you've learned and integrated so far is like driving a beat up car. It will get you from point A to point B, but without any style or elegance. A master practitioner has all the options that most drivers expect. You wouldn't buy a car without power steering or power locks, would you? Then, why would you expect someone to buy your services?" She signed up immediately.

CHAPTER 21:
USING ERICKSONIAN HYPNOSIS

At this point I should mention that there is a difference between conversational and Ericksonian hypnosis. I'm reminded of math class in grade school, where I learned that a square is a rectangle, but a rectangle is not a square, and both are parallelograms. In our context here, both of these approaches are styles of hypnosis, but each has unique characteristics. Conversational hypnosis is Ericksonian hypnosis, but the reverse is not necessarily true. Conversational hypnosis also includes the use of Sleight of Mouth Patterns, developed by Robert Dilts in 1999, which is explained in Part 7 of this volume. Additionally, Erickson would also pace a client's experience and then begin to lead them into trance (or downtime). So, when doing Ericksonian hypnosis, you will be employing the use of downtime to create a trance state in your client. This would not be appropriate in business or sales environments, so instead, use conversational hypnosis in those contexts.

The format Erickson used is as follows:

- Pace and lead.

- Distract the conscious mind.

- Speak directly to the unconscious and access its hidden resources.

PACING AND LEADING

To pace a client, begin by matching and mirroring her physiology, choice of words, tone of voice, etc., then make reference to what she would most likely be seeing, hearing, feeling or thinking (e.g. "As you notice the lights slowly dimming ..." or, "As you hear my voice ..." or, "As you feel the chair on your back..." or "As you wonder...") while speaking slowly in a soft tonality and pacing your speech to her breathing. To lead her into downtime, begin to focus her attention inward by saying something such as, "You may notice how easy it is to close your eyes whenever you wish to feel more relaxed..."

DISTRACT THE CONSCIOUS MIND.

Also known as bypassing the critical factor, distracting the conscious mind can be achieved in a variety of ways. Usually it is done using confusion, but it can also be accomplished through providing an overload of sensory information. One technique Milton would often use was to have the patient stare at a point on the wall while thinking of something that involved a lot of imagery.

Any successful hypnotic induction distracts the conscious mind. Using a multitude of hypnotic language patterns can create confusion and lead the conscious mind elsewhere. However you do it, the purpose of distraction is to get embedded and direct suggestions through to the unconscious.

SPEAK DIRECTLY TO THE UNCONSCIOUS AND ACCESS ITS HIDDEN RESOURCES.

Erickson believed that the unconscious mind stored all the resources needed to make positive changes. Therefore, his approach to therapy was to access those resources by finding a context in which they occurred. Anchoring is based on this concept. For example, if a person lacks confidence in asking someone on a date, you can lead them to access that feeling of confidence in another situation, and then you could apply it to asking for a date.

Another way Erickson accessed resources was through "gaining learning." By reviewing past events or imagining positive futures, the unconscious mind can gather learning that can be applied to the current situation. To continue with the above example, the client could be led back into the past to discover how he developed that lack of confidence and gather a new understanding that could shift his feelings in the present. Another option would be to have him imagine being able to ask someone out. After viewing this being done, he may change his belief in what he's able to do. Both options provide successful learning and belief changes.

THE UTILIZATION INDUCTION

Now that you understand what to do with a client in the hypnotic state, it's helpful to know exactly how to get them there. Milton Erickson used very different induction methods than most of his contemporaries. Because of his background with nonverbal communication, he would often build rapport and use it to take his patients into a trance state. He also employed utilization to either take them deeper or bypass their resistance to going into hypnosis.

The Utilization Induction is my favorite method for inducing trance, because it's quick, easy, and applicable to any situation. It's simple to master, especially since you have already learned all the elements involved. Let's put them together now so that you can start practicing.

USING RAPPORT

In hypnosis your ability to either link things together or pull them apart is increased. Therefore, you can use the hypnotic state to link any two things (or more) together. The utilization induction is based purely on the rapport relationship between you and the client. All you have to do is gain very deep rapport, begin to put yourself into a trance, and model the signs of trance for your client.

Steps to the Utilization Induction

1. State several things you know to be true in your subject's experience (2-3 in a row), then state one thing that leads toward hypnosis in a permissive way. Use Milton Model language patterns.
2. State several more things you know to be true in your subject's experience and follow with a statement about what you want to the client to do (still permissively).
3. Continue verbally pacing the subject's experience for several minutes, gradually becoming more direct in your suggestions. Here's an example:

"As you feel the temperature of the air on your skin, feel the weight of clothing on your body, and hear the sound of my voice you can relax deeply."

"While you breathe in and out, experiencing this moment, and feel your hands, you can go into a trance."

4. Any time the subject does what you suggest, say "that's right."
5. If you encounter resistance, reframe it as a positive experience, and suggest how it can deepen the trance.

Milton Erickson found that by pacing a client's experience a few times, he could link the feeling of "yes" to something he wanted the client to do. Similar to the "yes set" often employed in sales, it is, essentially, an anchored relationship between things that can be verified and things that cannot. The process gives credence to hypnotic suggestions that might otherwise be dismissed or caught by the conscious mind and discarded. In order for a new suggestion to be accepted by the unconscious, it must feel "right." After hearing several agreeable statements consecutively, a person is likely to also feel right about an unverifiable suggestion.

After you've given several rapport based suggestions, you can also use Utilization to bypass resistance. For example, if you've suggested that they eyes close and they haven't, you can use their resistance in a positive way. You may want to suggest that they have control over their eyes, and that means they will be able to accept only positive suggestions. Eventually the eyes will close, even if it is only to blink.

POSITIVE REINFORCEMENT

Another important consideration in doing hypnosis is making sure the subject can accept your suggestions. This can only happen if they are not second guessing everything they are experiencing. Many individuals that are new to hypnosis don't know exactly what to expect, and they are often nervous about getting it right. There is a simple way to bypass this type of resistance.

Erickson often used positive reinforcement to get around these challenges. If his subject took a breath when he asked her to, he'd say, "That's right." If she closed her eyes when he mentioned it, he would say, "Good." This reinforcement gives the subject a good feeling, and allows her to go much deeper, faster. And for a resistant client, as in the above example, eventually they will blink. You'll respond with, "That's right."

USING THE MILTON MODEL TO GIVE SUGGESTIONS

When doing Ericksonian hypnosis, remember to use the Milton Model language patterns. They are the structure for giving hypnotic suggestion in a permissive, allowing way. They also create confusion, which serves to deepen the trance and bypass the conscious mind.

If you plan to use Ericksonian techniques in the workplace, taking a person into deep hypnosis is not generally appropriate. Keep in mind that the Milton Model can be used in these settings to produce a light trance and get your positive suggestions through. Just leave out the hypnotic induction and you'll get the results you're after.

The best way to learn and integrate these processes is to practice them, over and over again. Start with just a couple of patterns, and use them in a variety of situations. Keep adding new ones, until you can put them all together. After a while, you'll be a master!   .

SUMMARY

Ericksonian Hypnosis is one the most fascinating and fun methods for doing trance work. It can be used in any situation, and I find the Milton Model to be the best tool I have ever learned. Understanding and using the language of influence and metaphors will open many doors for you, as it can improve your relationships, further your career, and ensure that others hear your great ideas. Remember, though, to always use it with integrity!

STUDY QUESTIONS

1. What is the value of inducing confusion in a hypnotic subject?
2. What are the benefits to using indirect suggestions?
3. Why is the goal of Ericksonian hypnosis to create rapport between the conscious and unconscious minds?
4. What are the fundamentals of Ericksonian hypnosis?
5. In what ways can utilization benefit your life and work?
6. What is the relationship between the Milton Model and the Meta Model?
7. What criteria need to be met in order for a metaphor to be considered therapeutic?

PART 6:
ADVANCED TECHNIQUES

Introduction:
Taking NLP to the Next Level

By this point, we've laid the foundation for practicing NLP. Now let's look at more advanced ways to employ the information you've learned. A practitioner of NLP is able to set anchors, work with parts, and utilize strategies and basic submodalities. A master practitioner can use the Milton Model, hypnotic regression, and advanced submodalities to make desired changes.

In this section you'll learn how to conduct an Ericksonian regression, which is often utilized to uncover and release past traumas. I'll also add finer distinctions to several tools, including anchoring and submodalities. I'll introduce more advanced patterns for making behavioral shifts and New Code NLP, designed by John Grinder. You'll learn how to bypass resistance to change by using a client's values to leverage against the behavior, by amplifying the outcome of avoiding change, and by using content-free techniques.

If you are planning on using NLP for difficult clients, such as those mandated for therapy or those that have been in traditional therapy for years, what you'll learn here will be most beneficial.

CHAPTER 22:
CONDUCTING A HYPNOTIC AGE
REGRESSION

Age regression is a way of accessing an individual's repressed memories. While this can be used to remember pleasant forgotten memories, more often it is employed to release a past emotional trauma. The unconscious mind represses memories to prevent emotional overload, or for protection. Repressed traumatic memories are only allowed by the unconscious to surface in a safe and controlled setting. If an individual relives an abusive scenario spontaneously or constantly it would grossly inhibit their ability to function. In these cases repression can be the best option. But, when the unconscious knows you're ready to deal with the trauma and its resulting emotions, it can serve up those memories for processing, learning, and resolution.

All of your memories are stored in the unconscious. Even if you cannot consciously remember something, there is a part of you that does. Using age regression to recall more mundane memories, like where you left your keys or being with a loved one can be a particularly useful tool. And, because this use of age regression is simple to learn and understand, in this chapter I will focus on resolving repressed memories.

Regression Elements

While there are several styles and methods for conducting regression, Milton Erickson's techniques form the basis of NLP. And regardless of which style you choose to implement, there are a few basics you need to know.

Using an Affect Bridge

By anchoring the un-resourceful emotion, you can open the emotional gestalt and locate the root cause of the presenting issue.

Begin by anchoring the problem emotion. Then, fire off the anchor while having your client move backwards along their timeline. Continue going further into the past until you hit the earliest memory in which the emotion is present.

Regressing To Root Cause

Every therapeutic regression aims to locate and resolve the root cause of the problem, which is the event that created the emotional issue. Memories are connected like links in a chain by a common thread that can be emotional, temporal, or situational, and known as a **gestalt**. Consider how you would determine what you were doing in June of 1992. Do you have a strong feeling that presents a particular memory? Do you go back chronologically, or do you think about where you lived, who you dated, etc? You can use any of these common threads to elicit memories contained within a gestalt.

Understanding a client's entire gestalt is crucial to resolving their past trauma. For example, if an individual has suffered abuse over a period of several years, she has likely developed a large gestalt of painful memories. In order to release all of her past negative emotion it's critical to resolve the root cause memory, as well as process all of the resulting emotions and memories. However, if your client has only one sensitizing event, your treatment will be fairly brief.

Getting to the root cause is not often difficult. There are a few techniques that are highly effective, particularly the affect bridge and the timeline. Once a client is in trance, it's very easy to elicit emotional states. The affect (or emotion) bridge technique utilizes the client's current emotional state to open the gestalt. Then it's just a matter of going back in time to the earliest experience of that emotion. Using a timeline is a linear method for going back chronologically to the root cause. It's simple and very effective, and it can be combined with the affect bridge.

Briefly mentioned in Part 4, timelines are our way of separating the past from the present and future. No doubt you encountered them in history class. When doing NLP, we use them as a regression tool, as well as a few other applications. By discovering and envisioning your personal timeline, you can easily slide into the past or out into the future to locate specific events or create imagined experiences.

PROCESSING THE MEMORY WITH ADVANCED SUBMODALITIES

Three-Place Dissociation

This is used for severely traumatic experiences to ensure the subject feels safe enough to be able to retrieve the memory.

This is done by anchoring the feelings of safety and comfort, as they imagine being in the projection booth of a movie theater, watching another version of them sitting in a seat in the theater, watching themselves in the memory on the screen.

The anchor for safety and comfort is held throughout the process, and it may need to be continually strengthened.

When using NLP for regression, it's necessary to shift problematic emotions and limiting beliefs that resulted from the root cause incident. There are two distinct ways to do this: using advanced submodalities or anchoring. In both scenarios, the object is to generate a catharsis, or a release of unpleasant emotions from the body.

You have already learned how to use anchoring, and I will explain further how to do so in the hypnotic state. First, though, let's identify two submodality distinctions used in NLP-based regression. You are already familiar with dissociation, and you know that it removes strong emotion. The second distinction is that individuals who hold on to negative emotion from a past event play the memory forward. However, when the memory is played backward the emotion changes, just like playing a tape backwards changes the sound you hear.

Milton Erickson often employed the use of dissociation with clients who had suffered severe traumas, because it reduces the emotional and physical pain present in the memory. When a trance subject is dissociated, safety and comfort can be easily maintained while viewing a past event. This is the essential concept utilized when working with allergies and phobias, which are described in the next chapter. To some extent, disassociation also changes the emotions linked to an event, because once it's viewed from a neutral place, the emotion present in the memory actually begins to lessen.

Systematic desensitization is a form of treatment in which a dissociated trance subject is moved progressively closer and closer, in their imagination, to the thing most feared. This process is often employed when working with fears and phobias, but it can also be applied to other traumas because there is almost always some fear involved. Some subjects are initially resistant to reliving a bad memory, so baby-stepping them closer to the memory from a neutral place is a good option.

There are several ways to dissociate a subject while in the hypnotic state. The easiest and most common is to use a movie theater as a metaphor. In this method, the client imagines sitting comfortably in the theater while watching a black and white movie of their memory. Keep in mind that imagination is heightened in hypnosis, so using imagined scenes is fairly simple. Another method is to look at the memory from a variety of angles, as if photographing the scene. I find that, while a little more challenging, this can be a more thorough way of ensuring dissociation. Remember that whenever you're dissociating someone, you must instruct them to see themselves in the memory, as opposed to seeing it from their own point of view. A third option I took from *A Christmas Carol.* I have the subject pretend they are their future selves visiting their past self. Most people know the story, and it's an obvious metaphor that is hard to miss.

The second main option for processing a traumatic memory is association to positive resources, or **re-anchoring**. This is usually more favorable than association without resources into the initial event. Even though many hypnotherapists employ that method with great results, it is often painful, unpleasant, and potentially dangerous. Unless you've received direct hypnotherapy training for dealing with abreactions, it is best to stick to associating into resources before taking a subject into a traumatic memory fully associated.

The major benefit of adding resources, including positive emotions and behavioral choices, is that it allows a subject to experience the event differently. For example, if someone remembers being a young child and having his toys taken away, and you regressed him back into that event, he's likely to experience the same emotions all over again. While an abreaction at this point can be therapeutic, it is usually unpleasant. If, however, you were to associate him into a feeling of calm acceptance, and then had him relive the memory, he is likely to respond with something like, "Oh well, I didn't really like those toys anyway. Where are the Cheerios?" That's a very different response, indeed!

By associating to resources and applying them to the initial event, not only does the response change, but the beliefs about the situation also change. The man above could change his belief from, "I never get to have what I want" to "I don't need to get bent out of shape every time something disappears from my life, because maybe I didn't really want it." Since beliefs govern our future actions, changing limiting beliefs is a top priority.

While associating into positive resources is therapeutic in itself, in most cases I recommend associating into the root cause memory with the resources. This ensures a catharsis and generally leads to the belief changes noted above. When conducting regression, I consider the belief change to be critical, even in the case of phobias. The last thing you want is for the subject to emerge from trance still believing the problem exists and thinking the same way as before you started. This can undermine your work and leave the subject confused.

When associating someone into a root cause event, it is also important to use Ericksonian language patterns to suggest further learning and change. One way Erickson would do this was to suggest that the subject be able to remember what happened in the past without having the negative emotion attached to it. In one example he said, "As you review that, you can now experience an appropriate balance between thinking and feeling about the whole thing."

Processing the Gestalt

Once the initial sensitizing event has been changed, it is important to process the rest of the memories in that Gestalt. In the case of phobias, there might only be one event, but in most situations there are several. It is not always necessary to process each situation differently, but applying the learning from the first event is crucial to ensuring each subsequent event is also changed appropriately.

Applying the Change to the Current and Future Contexts

Once you've changed the emotions in the memory and the client has formed new, positive beliefs and applied them to the entire gestalt, it's time to apply the learning to the context in which the problem used to occur. At this point you have several options. The way I prefer to proceed is with an anchor collapse. Then I lead the client through changing their behaviors in the future. By changing both the emotion and the behavior in the current situation, and by affirming the new beliefs they have formed, you are ensuring the change will be generative.

As mentioned previously, future pacing your work is always necessary. Every time I conduct a regression I have the subject associate into every possible context that's relevant to their situation. If there are dozens, as in the case of smoking, I will have them imagine going through their whole day very quickly, focusing on the most difficult spots. Then I will lead them through a week, a month, and a year. Usually this covers enough situations. For specific situations they find particularly difficult, I will future pace those several times to ensure the unconscious has correctly applied the change.

Dealing with Past Life Memories

While Past Life Regression is not specifically addressed within the realms of NLP, occasionally a subject will drop into a past life memory when regressed. This is not common, but it does happen, especially if they believe in reincarnation. If this occurs, whether or not you believe it yourself, treat the memory as if it is real. Keep in mind that it may be serving as a metaphor for their transformation. Not every individual is ready or able to deal with the actual memory consciously, so they generate a story to get the learning and make the change.

If a past life memory does come up, the processing is slightly different than working with a single childhood memory. Often you will have to process the entire lifetime, including the death scene, in order to change the emotions and beliefs. This is due to the possibility that the subject will not go instantly to the sensitizing event; they go to a neutral place in that lifetime first to acclimate to the memory. When this happens, you may need to fast forward to the trauma. But, if the subject goes to a traumatic past life memory initially, process it as usual. For more information on conducting this type of regression, refer to the index.

CHAPTER 23:
WORKING WITH PHOBIAS

One thing that has made NLP so popular with therapists the world over is the successful treatment of phobias. No other form of treatment works as quickly or as thoroughly as NLP for these types of fears.

A phobia is defined as an irrational, overwhelming fear of an object or situation that poses little or no actual danger. A phobia might seem like a typical fear, yet a phobia has an excessive and unreasonable desire to avoid the feared subject. Most fears can be overcome and faced without therapeutic intervention. A phobia cannot. According the National Institute of Mental Health, about 15% of Americans suffer from phobias, the most common form of mental illness in women and the second most common in men.

TYPES OF PHOBIAS

Phobias are divided into three categories; social phobias, specific phobias, and agoraphobia. Social phobias are linked with anxiety, as in the case of public speaking or performance anxiety. These types of phobias are multifaceted and require treatment of both the actual phobia and the anxiety. Specific phobias are the most common type and include fears of dogs, snakes, water, elevators, and other objects. These are the easiest phobias to treat, as they are usually just cause-and-effect conditioning. Agoraphobia is probably the most difficult to treat, because people that suffer from this type of anxiety disorder are often unable to feel safe anywhere but in their own home. They commonly suffer from panic attacks in public places and groups. Some agoraphobics end up homebound because of their fears.

Despite the level of difficulty involved in working with some types of phobias, all are treatable. Once you understand that phobias arise from an initial sensitizing event that has become generalized to anything closely resembling the object encountered in that event, all that is required is to process the event (possibly through regression) and apply that change to all the contexts in which the fear occurs.

MOST COMMON PHOBIAS

While there are dozens of phobias that exist, a few of the most common ones have been identified. I once commented in a class that the most common specific phobias are of public speaking and flying, and someone could build an entire practice on working with just those phobias. Someone took me up on that and has created a very successful business working with corporate employees that travel and give presentations. I'm sure there are many more opportunities like this out there for a motivated individual.

Some other common phobias are arachnophobia, or fear of spiders, claustrophobia, a fear of confined spaces, and acrophobia, a fear of heights. In truth, people with acrophobia aren't afraid of heights; they are afraid of falling or being injured. One phobia most people are unaware of is emetophobia, or fear of vomiting, which is surprisingly common.

Try this at Home: Clearing a Phobia

1. Access phobic state and calibrate.
2. Establish three-place dissociation.
3. Access the initial sensitizing event.
4. Run the movie of the original experience in black and white, while staying dissociated. Gather any relevant learning, if necessary.
5. Associate into the last frame of the movie, when you're safe again, and run the movie backwards.
6. Imagine the thing of which you were phobic. Ensure the fear is gone. If not, repeat steps 4 and 5 until the emotion releases fully.

Before working with specific phobias, do a little research to determine their structure. Each phobia has at least one internal representation, which has a specific set of submodalities. If you know how an individual represents their phobia (the picture is too big, the sound is too loud, etc), you will know what to change. For example, acrophobics tend to visually distort their surroundings by taking in too much information. This often leads to confusion and dizziness. I have found it very useful to reduce the brightness and size and make the image stationary. This puts the actual height in proper perspective. Keep in mind, though, to always determine each person's submodalities, because these can be different for each individual.

WORKING WITH SOCIAL PHOBIAS

Having personally suffered from a social phobia as a child, I have a preference for working with these types of intense fears. I know how pervasive and tricky they can be, but after having successfully resolved one for myself, I have found several useful techniques.

In the case of public speaking, which is where I experienced difficulty, most individuals develop their fear over time. Common initial sensitizing events include being teased by classmates, receiving poor feedback from teachers, giving the wrong answer when called on in class, or being raised by domineering parents or other close adults. Most likely, the fear got stronger with each event, eventually morphing into a phobia. Symptoms of this phobia include excessive sweating, the mind "going blank," an increased heart rate, and even fainting. Because most individuals with this type of phobia avoid public speaking, their career opportunities can be limited.

Social phobias have two components to them, so there is an added step to the Phobia Process noted in the insert. Commonly, anxiety results from a lack of certainty. To resolve this, you will need to generate certainty by future pacing extensively, as well as having the client test their results in the real world. And since there are likely to be several sensitizing events, you may have to run a process on each event, gathering new learning and new beliefs from each. In my case, I had a few examples of being pressured to speak up when I believed I had nothing of value to say in the situation. When I visited those events, I realized that I needed to learn how to speak up for myself and feel confident enough to know I had something valuable to say. Once I did that, I began teaching NLP, something I consider to be very valuable.

Once the learning is gathered, beliefs are changed, and emotional resources are anchored and attached to all relevant contexts, you are ready to rewind the initial sensitizing experiences. This will disconnect the unpleasant emotion from the event, freeing the individual to create a new reality. And when you future pace these changes by firing off the resource anchors in every possible context and install the new beliefs (by linking positive emotion to them), your success rate will surprise even you.

WORKING WITH SPECIFIC PHOBIAS

As mentioned previously, specific phobias are the easiest to release. Most can be done in an hour or two. I've even witnessed a few being released in less than fifteen minutes! This is because specific phobias all have the same structure: x causes y. Seeing a spider (x) causes the immediate reaction of fear (y). With these phobias, you can change the content of the strategy (seeing a spider and reacting with curiosity) while maintaining the structure (x causes y). All you need to do to resolve specific phobias is to change the response (y). Remember, these simple strategies are the most effective.

When clearing specific phobias, I also find it very useful to reframe the client's experience, mostly because many phobics believe their phobias will be very difficult to change. They believe this because their physical and emotional experience is intense, but you know differently. So tell them. Here are a couple of reframes I use with my clients.

"Most people learned to be phobic in a single experience that either or seemed to be dangerous. And because you learned to be phobic from this single experience, you were able to do what psychologists call 'one-trial learning,' and that ability to learn quickly will make it easy for you to learn a new response just as quickly."

"The part of you that has been maintaining this fear to protect you all these years is important and valuable, and you want to preserve its ability to keep you safe in dangerous situations. All you want to do now is refine and improve its ability to protect you in a more pleasant and useful way."

Once you've delivered these reframes, all that is left is to process the root cause, as in the pattern listed in the inset. In some instances, you will need to future pace using systematic desensitization. Test how close the individual can get to the feared object before panic sets in. Keep in mind that the point is not to get a person with a phobia of snakes to pick up a rattlesnake; that would be dangerous. What you're aiming for is for them to feel comfortable encountering one in the wild, while responding in the most appropriate fashion (like walking away carefully). Make sure you determine the appropriate response before future pacing so you don't sabotage the process.

I have personally worked with several arachnophobes in my career, possibly because I teach classes in California and Arizona, two places known for large spiders. I don't have a fear of spiders, but I'm not likely to just go and pick one up. But that is exactly what I had to do one day. A client I worked with was phobic of tarantulas, and I was in Sedona giving a seminar. The wall outside the training room often had one clinging to it in the early morning and at dusk. My client would only allow me to work on his fear if I proved the process would work. So, in order to help him, I quickly ran the phobia process on myself and picked up the biggest spider I have ever seen. And, about ten minutes later, so did my client. It was a very exciting experience, and one I don't plan to repeat any time soon!

Since that time, I have used the phobia process to fire walk, cliff dive, swim with sting rays, and after crashing in an ultra-lite plane (to avoid developing a fear). It's a great resource to have.

WORKING WITH AGORAPHOBIA

Try this at Home: Changing Beliefs
1. Elicit submodalities of the limiting belief.
2. Elicit submodalities of something not believed.
3. Change the submodalities of the limiting belief to match the representation of what is not believed.
4. Break the state.
5. Test by having the person state the new belief. Does it feel true?

Agoraphobia is defined as a fear of not being able to escape, and it is commonly confused as being a fear of open places. Most agoraphobics have difficulty in places from which they can't easily escape, and their symptoms run from mild to severe. A person with mild agoraphobia may be able to go out in public places but will always have in mind a clear escape plan. People with more severe symptoms may never leave the house.

Working with agoraphobia takes longer and is more difficult than resolving specific phobias, mostly because of the level of anxiety that is present. There is only one definite way to get rid of agoraphobia; you have to deal with the thought patterns that trigger the fear. By now you know thoughts are internal representations, whether visual, auditory, or kinesthetic. Many agoraphobics have representations in each modality, which compounds the issue.

To permanently change a person's thoughts, you have to change the submodalities of each trigger representation. You can do this by using the Phobia Process listed in the insert. If the individual has a belief that danger is present when it isn't, you will also have to shift the submodalities of the representation of that belief by matching them to the submodalities of something they do not believe (see Changing Beliefs insert). This may need to be repeated by all limiting beliefs involved.

After the trigger representations have been dealt with, you'll also need to address the behavioral aspects of agoraphobia. After anchoring safety and confidence, have the individual imagine being able to easily go out in public and crowded places. This changes their visceral experience and builds the belief they are improving. You may also need to reframe the belief that they need an escape plan.

If there is any residue after completing all of the processes listed above, there may also be an element of low self confidence and a lack of courage. I find that teaching the client how to laugh at themselves with true acceptance is a great option here. If they laugh every time they think about needing to escape, they can't feel fear.

MORE CONSIDERATIONS

In a few cases I have had to use a role model to assist my client in determining how to respond appropriately to the thing they fear. This is described in detail in Part 8 of this book, but for our purposes here, just select someone that responds in safe and reasonable way to the thing they fear. I used to use Steve Irwin, the Crocodile Hunter, but, sadly, that's not a good option anymore. He was also too extreme for most people anyway. The best role models for dealing with phobias are people that can remain calm, curious, and rational. Find someone that will look at a poisonous snake, interested in it, but not feel the need to pick it up.

Another option for stubborn phobias is to utilize confusion. I like to think of this as scrambling the circuits in their brain so that the phobic individual "forgets" how to be phobic. Remember, every phobia has a specific strategy, or sequence of events that lead to the panic reaction. If you change the size of the spider, the movement (moving away instead of towards), and the speed at which it moves several times, eventually confusion will set in, and the individual will be unable to maintain the fear.

CHAPTER 24:
CONTENT-FREE TECHNIQUES

Occasionally I get clients that are uncomfortable talking about their issues, due to embarrassment or fear of being "outed" in their community. Despite my assurances of confidentiality, there are a few folks that just won't cave. Additionally, NLP was originally developed as content-free therapy, focusing on process over content, or the "how" over the "what." In recent years, however, some content has leaked in, partially due to modeling. NLP is anything that works, and a few NLP modelers have found situations in which content is helpful. In either case, there are some major advantages to using content-free techniques.

Content-free processes ensure that neither you nor your client get too involved in the back story, as often occurs in traditional talk therapy. When doing NLP, we aren't too concerned with what happened in the past, and after some of the stories I've heard I've become hypnotized by the client, eventually feeling that their issue is too difficult to resolve! I hope I don't have to tell you this is NOT what we want to happen. By processing the issue without listening to the whole sob story, you can stay resourceful for your client.

Try this at Home- Sliding Anchors

1. Generate a really strong, pleasant feeling by remembering a past event. Strengthen it using submodalities.
2. Anchor the state with one finger on the inside of your forearm.
3. Break the state and test your anchor.
4. Then, slide your finger from the anchored spot in an upwards direction (towards your heart). Imagine a sound with an upward pitch as you move your finger. I like to use the sound of an airplane taking off. Notice how the feeling gets stronger.
5. To decrease the intensity of the state, slide the finger in the other direction while you lower your pitch.
6. Imagine a situation in which this feeling would be useful. Fire the anchor and slide it upwards. Notice how different the situation feels.

Besides avoiding possible embarrassment, another advantage to this approach is that it keeps the client from hypnotizing themselves further. I find that the more a person has talked about the problem, the bigger and more real it seems to them. The last thing you want to do is have them create another memory of the problem!

A number of processes in this volume can be done with little to no information as to the client's story. Even the information gathering process can be done without the practitioner knowing the answers to their questions. The important thing is that the client knows what they want, can envision it, and feels confident they can overcome any blocks to having it. All of the work is being done in the client's mind anyway, so it's very easy to guide them through the process without needing to know exactly what they are doing. Keep in mind though, that you'll need to check in regularly with the client to ensure they're following along in an appropriate way. This is possible for you to do at this point, because you have learned to calibrate nonverbal communication, and you have the language skills to direct an individual through a process using indirect suggestions and persuasive language that prompts them to make the change. You will need to practice these skills to be truly efficient at content-free techniques.

SLIDING ANCHORS

Sliding Anchors are used to amplify and decrease the intensity of an emotional state. Richard Bandler often combines sliding anchors with stacking to create pleasurable intense states. Anchoring, in general, is a content-free technique. The subject is free to take the emotion into the problematic situation without needing to tell you what that situation is.

I like using sliding anchors, mostly because they're fun to play with. They function in much the same way as traditional anchoring, but they have the added value of sound and sensation to change the intensity of the state.

PATTERN INTERRUPTS

Your internal strategies are always running. But sometimes the strategies you run create results you don't like. These patterns can be changed, but in order to do so, you've got to change your internal state quickly. For example, a phobia is a two-step strategy; stimulus and response. To break that pattern, you've got to intercede the moment the stimulus is triggered. Otherwise, the fear response will already be up and running.

To break a pattern you have to prevent the trigger from producing the undesired response. Because strategies run so quickly, as a practitioner you have to be prepared. I once had a client with an allergy to temperature changes, and when I asked him how he produced the hives that would develop on his body, his eyes moved down as he indicated a sensation at the top of his head. As soon as that sensation began, it quickly moved down his body. Moments later, he'd get red and start to develop patches on his skin. Because I had been paying attention to his eye movements and nonverbal communications, I knew that I had to intercede between the trigger (temperature change) and the response (sensation on his head). So I asked him again how he developed the hives. As soon as he looked down, I shouted, "Woohoo!" He looked confused, but he trusted me enough to continue. I asked him again to produce the hives, and again I shouted. After a couple of times he just started laughing. He could no longer create the sensation, and the hives disappeared from his life.

Now, not all pattern interrupts require you to act bizarrely. However, if you have rapport, you can get away with a lot. But sometimes a more subtle approach is needed. I first learned Betty Erickson's Self Hypnosis technique in an NLP workshop, and I fell in love with it immediately. I quickly realized it could apply quite well to a therapeutic outcome. Instead of using it to go into trance, I like to use it to disrupt a link between a bad feeling and a particular situation, similar to an anchor collapse.

Try this at Home: Overcoming Overwhelming Emotions
1. Identify an emotionally sensitive issue.
2. Think or say one thing about the issue that is bothersome. As soon as the negative emotion comes up, take a deep breath.
3. Bring your awareness to something you can see in the environment around you. Then note something you can hear. Keep doing this until the emotion fades.
4. Then, think or say one more thing that is bothering you about the issue. As soon as the negative emotion comes up, take a deep breath.
5. Bring your awareness to something you can see in the environment around you. Then note a sensation in your body, like the feel of your clothing. Keep doing this until the emotion fades.
6. Repeat these steps until you can no longer access any negative emotion about the situation. You can mix up the sensory systems in any combination you desire, using smell and taste if you desire.

Other NLP masters have created similar techniques to keep an individual present in their environment so that they will be unable to retrieve negative feelings. One process for assisting an individual to stay present in a good state, instead of accessing painful emotions and memories, is extremely effective and can be used repeatedly to help a client become more present in their bodies and in their lives.

My take on this process is particularly useful for clients that tend to get stuck in bad feelings, creating an inability to get to a solution. I call this "circular reasoning," and it is often associated with depression and anxiety. It's fast, simple, and effective. I have used it many times with phone clients, mostly because it is content free and keeps them from going down the tubes when thinking about their problem.

There are a variety of ways to break a pattern and establish clearer thinking. John Grinder has developed a method called *The Alphabet Game* that involves moving the body while saying the alphabet aloud. It aligns the left and right hemispheres of the brain, which is helpful when making decisions, because it gives you access to all the resources you have inside. I invite you to create your own technique.

CHANGING THE TIMELINE

Another great content-free technique commonly used for improving many areas of life is changing the timeline. As you know, a timeline is a way to sort the past, present, and future. Occasionally there are issues with the timeline itself (as opposed to problematic memories on the timeline), and these distortions can disrupt your happiness and success. Take the quiz below to determine how your timeline is working for you.

Quiz: Is your timeline working for you?

- Are you consistently running late?
- Do you have difficulty planning for the future?
- Are you afraid of the future?
- Do you often feel stuck in the past, or do you have difficulty changing?
- Do you feel short on time, never having enough to get things done?
- Do you have gaps in your memory?
- Do you have difficulty in imagining your future being different or better?

If you answered yes to any of the questions, you may have a problem with your timeline. So, let's determine what to do about it.

TIMELINE ORIENTATION

There are two main **timeline** orientations: in time and through time. An in-time timeline is an associated time line; a through-time orientation is a dissociated timeline. To determine how your line is positioned, you can remember specific events and notice where those memories are located in space. One way to know where they are located is to notice where your eyes move when you remember the event. So, think about putting your shoes on yesterday. Now, point to that experience. Then, think about putting on your shoes tomorrow. Point to that as well. Then, consider putting on your shoes now and notice where that experience is located. Then, draw an imaginary line connecting those experiences, keeping in mind that it may not be a straight line. This is your timeline. If you have difficulty finding an experience in space, check if it is behind you.

Here are a few more ways to determine timeline orientation:

- Eye movements

- Body movements, particularly gestures

- Pointing to an emotionless experience.

Most timelines orient either left to right, with "now" being about 12 inches in front the body, or front to back, with "now" being inside the body. Of course there are variations of this, but most timelines will fit one of these orientations. Some common variations include U shaped lines, V shaped lines, spirals, and up/down lines. Some orientations I have encountered that are problematic orient with the past in front and the future in back, overlapping pasts and futures, and scattered experiences that don't form a line. Usually these orientations belie more serious issues, and simply fixing the line isn't enough to create lasting change.

To change your timeline orientation to one that could work better for you, just imagine floating up above your timeline. Then, watch your timeline change to the orientation you desire. Take the time to notice all the distinctions that shift. When the timeline is as you desire, float down into your body and lock the new timeline in place. Over the next few days, intentionally place experiences where they "belong" on your timeline. After a few days, experiences will naturally go to their new locations.

SUBMODALITIES OF THE TIMELINE

You already understand the importance of submodalities in regards to how they affect your feelings, but you may not yet realize that they also apply to your timeline. How you represent your past, present, and future has an effect on how you experience life.

ASSOCIATION AND DISSOCIATION

If you tend to consistently run late you likely have an in-time, or associated, timeline. This is a great vacation strategy, because it gives you the opportunity to fully enjoy the present moment. This a common orientation for artists and musicians, because those careers benefit from experiencing emotion and being present. I also see this orientation in computer programmers, who often work for hours on end, oblivious of the passage of time. The other option for running late is that your timeline is not calibrated correctly. I have a friend that was always exactly 15 minutes late to events. I adjusted her timeline by moving "now" fifteen minutes earlier on her line. She's been consistently on time since, barring traffic outside of her control.

On the flip side, if you are always on time and find it easy to schedule your time you likely have a through-time timeline. When you are dissociated from time, it is easier to see time in terms of distance. This orientation leads to a greater sense of the passing of time. This is NOT useful when you're standing in line, having sex, or writing a book. If you're having difficulty enjoying the moment or are often thinking rather than feeling what's going on around you, you're likely oriented through-time.

Most people switch back and forth between these orientations, and that is the best use of resources. And, now that you know that both orientations exist, you can adjust at will. Just imagine how your timeline is oriented in the moment, imagine grabbing hold of it, and move it in the direction you want it to go. Lock it in with a sealing sound, and you're all ready to go!

SHAPE

Many years ago, I came across an excellent book called *Change Your Mind – And Keep the Change* by Connirae and Steve Andreas. As I was reading I got an insight that completely changed my business. I had been having difficulty remembering when to send out email notices about upcoming classes. I offered early bird discounts for people that registered a month in advance, and I knew that I had to send a reminder about the deadline at least a week before. But, somehow, I would remember on the date of the deadline. As you might imagine, this didn't give people enough warning, and early registrations were lower than expected.

What I realized when I elicited my future timeline was that I could see clearly one, two, three, four, and six weeks in the future. Oops! I was missing week five, and that was when I needed to send the notices. So, I floated above my timeline and discovered that week 5 looked like a valley, so I pulled on the future and leveled it all out. From then on, my students got their emails on time.

COLOR, MOVEMENT, AND BRIGHTNESS

Another common timeline submodality issue regards color and brightness. How would you feel about your future if your future timeline was short, dark, and hazy. On the other hand, if your future timeline was long, bright, and sparkling, wouldn't you be overjoyed by the possibilities ahead of you?

What about the past or present? Does it look dark and depressing, or is it bright and full of great experiences? You could, you know, brighten up the dark patches so that you remember your past fondly or experience your current moments in a lighter way. But, please keep in mind, that timeline changes are incomplete unless you resolve the major issues in your past.

MULTIPLE TIMELINES

I once had a client that was completely stuck in her life and in her career. She had been doing the same job for 30 years, and she didn't even like it. After talking with her for some time, I found that her greatest joy was telling stories to her grandchildren. She had dozens of great stories to tell from her past. The only problem was that after telling them she felt depressed. She came to me to figure out how to move forward in her life. I quickly realized that she had a lot of pain in her past, mostly stemming from intense emotional abuse in her early childhood. We processed those memories, but she still didn't change in the way she had hoped.

One day I asked her about her future, and I noticed that her eyes looked into the past. It was a great "aha!" moment, as I realized that her past and future were overlapped! I surmised this had happened so that she could remember her stories. She had placed both her past and her future directly in front of her. It's obvious to me now that every time she thought about moving forward, all she could see was where she had been.

So, what did I do? I didn't want to disrupt her stories, so I left them on a line in front of her, slightly to her left. She would still be able to see them clearly, without them clouding her future. All of the unpleasant memories I placed on a separate line that we slid gently behind her. Since we had already processed those memories, it was safe to do this. And, we left the future in front of her, made it wider, brighter, and added some movement. A few months later I received a card from her. She had moved, taken a new job, and was happy for the first time in many years.

You can create multiple pasts and futures. Have fun exploring all the possibilities available when working with timelines!

SUMMARY

There is a lot of nuance involved in practicing NLP. There is also a great amount of creativity that you can tap into when working with the techniques you've learned. In this section I have you several ideas that myself and other NLP modelers and trainers have developed. They are by no means complete. There is plenty of room for your own developments, and I highly encourage you to explore each concept further.

Now that you've completed this section, consider how you can utilize this information in your own life and work. Move your timeline around, interrupt your limiting patterns, and change any of your fears and phobias. Your life will not be the same- it will be much, much better, brighter, and full of success.

STUDY QUESTIONS

1. How is association and dissociation used in regression therapy?
2. What are the differences between specific phobias and social phobias? What are the differences in how you treat them?
3. How, specifically, do you add resources to a memory in order to release negative emotion?
4. What is a pattern interrupt, and how can it be used to break an anchor?
5. List 3 submodality changes you can make to a timeline and how those changes will affect an individual's daily experience.

PART 7:
PRESENTATION SKILLS

INTRODUCTION:
THE KEYS TO POWERFUL
PRESENTATIONS

How many times have you watched someone on stage draw an audience into the world of the story they're telling? It's a magical moment when everything else disappears and you're transported into a specific place of that person's creation. Suddenly, it's just you and them, and all the emotions they wish to convey, the laughter or tears that emerge give you an experience that transcends time and space. And, of course, you remember it well.

Unfortunately, not everyone believes they have the capability to produce these results. But, because you are reading this now, you have hope that you can improve your ability to present your ideas, your skills, and your products more effectively. This section will give you what you need to be able to do just that. Whether you are on the stage or in the boardroom, you present yourself every day. Are you being as effective as you want to be?

There are really only three facets to giving excellent presentations: being fearless, having great content, and accurately conveying your message. You have to develop yourself on the inside and present yourself on the outside. For that reason, I've divided this section into three chapters; the first deals with your internal state, the second focuses on what to do with your body and voice, and the third chapter highlights the secrets of powerful presentations. On with it!

CHAPTER 26:
BEING FEARLESS

I've had the opportunity to witness some excellent speakers, sales professionals, and entertainers, and here I will distill their secrets for you. But first, let's deal with the most common barrier to giving great presentations- fear.

Fear rears its ugly head in a variety of ways. It can encourage you to clean out the sock drawer rather than make a few cold calls. It may cause you to forget what you had planned to say to an audience. Occasionally it will even make you sweat profusely. None of these results are going to provide you with more success in your life, so let's take some time to eliminate any fear you may have, hidden or apparent.

BEING RELAXED AND COMFORTABLE

Not every individual is afraid of speaking in public. Many people thrive in this environment, and not because they have the elusive "charisma gene." They merely have learned how to feel at ease in front of groups. A certain amount of anxiety is expected, but the ability to transform that anxiety into motivation to try harder is the hallmark of a great presenter.

Consider the example of individuals on reality shows like *American Idol* or *So You Think You Can Dance*. The contestants are often extremely nervous before they perform. However, their routines are so precise, and they've rehearsed so many times that once they step on the stage there is no room for fear. They often reframe their own beliefs by recognizing it isn't fear at all – it's excitement! Then they use that energy to perform at their very best.

The thing is, if there are people on the planet that can conquer the fear of public speaking, so can you. First, allow yourself to entertain the idea that you could be very comfortable giving lectures or selling your ideas to groups or individuals. Then, imagine doing it successfully. You'll find yourself getting much more open to the idea after just a few minutes.

I learned a lot by training as a dancer when I was young. I never once got on stage without being nervous, but my instructors gave me great advice. They reminded us all the night before the show that we were not there to strive for perfection. You can't control everything. No matter how much you practice, a shoe can fly off in the middle of a performance, the music can cut out, or you can have a wardrobe malfunction. These things cannot be controlled. So, go out and do your very best. Accept everything that happens with grace and maturity. The audience will respect you for making the best of the situation.

So, don't worry about being perfect. If you get tongue-tied, so what? What's the worst that's going to happen? If you skip something you wanted to say, go back and say it. The world is not going to end. Remember, the secret to a great life isn't what happens, but what you do with what happens. Practice humility, and learn how to laugh at yourself.

GETTING OVER YOUR FEAR OF PUBLIC SPEAKING

In poll after poll, public speaking tops the list as the most common fear, beating even fear of death. The most recent statistics show 40% of Americans report fear of public speaking. And, with numbers like that, it's no surprise most people could use some help when it comes to presentation skills.

Most fears are triggered by being exposed to the thing feared. However, public speaking fears are not only triggered by actually speaking in front of other people, anxiety can be produced by merely thinking about speaking to a group. This makes them a little more complex than other fears, but that does not mean they are impossible to overcome. Let's focus on the anxiety part first. Then we'll deal with the fear that's triggered during a presentation.

Even the most seasoned presenters occasionally have bouts of anxiety when preparing to give a talk. Some of the usual suspects for generating anxiety are presenting new material, speaking to unknown individuals, and feeling pressured to perform. In any case, the important thing to understand is that anxiety is often a message from the unconscious. Sometimes it wants you to make sure you're prepared, and other times it is reminding you to focus on your outcome. Other times there is no usefulness at all; you may be talking yourself into it.

To determine what's triggering your anxiety, ask the part of you what it's gaining from making you anxious. Then, find a way to resolve the issue, maybe by tweaking your presentation or getting to know your audience. If there doesn't seem to be any message or benefit from having the anxiety, you know it's just a simple issue of how you're thinking about the presentation. You may need to change your internal representation to reduce the impact it is having on you, by changing the tonality of your internal dialogue or seeing an image of things going well rather than an image of your talk tanking.

Try this at Home- Becoming a Confident Speaker

1. Imagine yourself on a white movie screen feeling relaxed, focused, and in charge. This means you're feeling confident and comfortable.
2. Watch your body language, particularly your posture and gestures. Notice your breathing rate and rate of speech.
3. Step into that version of you, allowing yourself to feel all the feelings of confidence, relaxation, and focus.
4. Pretend to be that person when giving your presentation. See it, feel it, and hear yourself speaking with a confident and relaxed tone.
5. Imagine the entire presentation going well, getting good feedback, and how great you feel once you're done.

In my experience, visualizing the audience in their underwear does nothing to diminish anxiety. What does, however, is making sure what you're seeing in your mind's eye is what you want, rather than what you don't want, and to scale. If the image is too big, you may feel like there are too many people. If it's too small, you won't consider it important enough. If it's too close to your face it may be overwhelming, and if it is too far away you may not treat it as urgent. Too much movement could also be a problem. So, be sure to check these submodalities for optimal results.

Another way to change the anxiety is to attach really good feelings to your representation. This is probably the easiest and most effective method. Above is a short exercise you can do to change it right now.

Once you've dealt with anything the fear was trying to convey to you and you've imagined the scene differently, you're ready to tackle the actual fear that comes up when you're delivering your presentation.

Remember the phobia process covered in Part 5? Right now, take twenty minutes, and guide yourself through that process to clear the root cause of your public speaking fear. Make sure to access the actual sensations you feel when you have to present, and use them to find the initial event that caused the fear. Public speaking fear is different from general fears, so you will need to identify the specific feelings you experience in order to be fully successful.

DEVELOPING YOUR PRESENTER STATE

Your internal state is the most important factor in how your audience responds to you. If you're nervous, your audience will feel nervous too. You may already know how important it is to remain centered, relaxed, and in control. But, how do you do that?

Your personal presenter state should be determined by the type of presentation you give. If you're in sales, then you may want to be confident and sincere. If you give lectures, you may want to be inspiring and passionate. Richard Bandler recommends the "your ass is mine" state for NLP and hypnotherapy trainers, mostly because it requires a great deal of confidence to demonstrate processes in front of an audience. Consider what would work best for your situation before proceeding to the exercise below.

First, consider what you always have available to you when you give your presentations. For me, I always wear a lapel microphone. Maybe you always turn on a projector or shake hands with decision makers. You can also use an auditory anchor, like a piece of music. This is a great option, because you can hear it in your own head. Consider a horn fanfare or a drum roll; they're fun and appropriate. Whatever you choose, this unique stimulus will become an anchor for you to enter your presenter state.

1. Decide what internal states you most want to hold when you speak (i.e. confidence, excitement, peace, etc).
2. One at a time, generate those states and anchor them to your unique trigger.
3. Employ the trigger to ensure the states are generated.
4. Practice using your trigger and recreating your state a couple of times to secure it.
5. Now, imagine you're about to give a presentation. Fire off your anchor and give a 3 minute presentation. Repeat this in 3 different situations (board room, stage, classroom, etc) to generalize your anchor to a variety of venues.

CHAPTER 27:
QUALITIES OF GREAT SPEAKERS

Every great speaker I have ever heard has a special, magical quality I call Charisma. Charisma is the ability to attract, inspire, and influence people. For many individuals, charisma is elusive, but there are specific elements that can be learned and incorporated into your speaking style that will increase your personal magnetism. This chapter will focus almost entirely on developing charisma. Additionally, you'll learn how to engage the audience, how to develop appropriate posture and voice quality, and how to generate specific emotional states in a group.

ENGAGING THE AUDIENCE

When it comes to public speaking, engaging the audience is your prime directive. As long as people are listening and paying attention, your talk is successful. If not, you're likely to bomb. Luckily, there are a few very simple techniques you can use to draw in the crowd.

- Looking at the audience
- Building rapport with the audience
- Telling stories
- Using humor

BUILDING RAPPORT WITH A GROUP

Building Group Rapport

- Rhythmic music
- Breathe together
- Laugh together
- Clap as a group
- Speak at a steady pace
- Drum beats

When speaking to an audience, it's helpful to make everyone in the room feel like you're speaking directly to them. One way to do this is to look at them! Too many presenters look at their feet or their notes, creating a barrier between them and the audience. Secondly, use a variety of visual, auditory, and kinesthetic predicates (sensory words) to build rapport. Some simple ways to get a group in rapport is to use music with a steady beat, have the group breathe together, speak at a steady rhythm, or get everyone laughing, clapping, or crying together. You can also build rapport by pacing their experiences. Below is one example of this. Feel free to modify it to fit your audience.

You've all come from different places. You've come up with the money and time off to be here. You've made arrangements for things to be handled while you're here learning something new. So, I'm going to give you my very best to ensure all of your efforts have been worth it.

Also, remember that the main objective in your presentation is not simply to get them to like you, but to get them to listen to you. By building rapport, they will naturally be inclined to listen, especially when you utilize some of the other techniques listed here.

Another way to build rapport with your listeners is to be yourself. I have found that humility and openness sets the stage for others to open up to you. I'm known to teach others about my mistakes, and what I learned from them. This has shown my students that even the pros make mistakes, and that mistakes are not a reason to give up. It also gives them the opportunity to discover how to learn from and overcome their own limitations. Of course, this is not a good idea in every context. When opening yourself up in this way, you often open the floodgates of sharing. Sometimes it can turn a lecture into a support group. Obviously, this is not a good tactic when giving a business presentation unless you do it quickly and offer a solution – yours.

Great performers and lecturers often consider their audience to be warm and friendly, not cold and prickly. Think about that for a moment. If every time you went to make a cold call and you assumed they were just waiting for your call, wouldn't it be easier to pick up the phone? Give your audience a little credit. They probably really want you to succeed. With this in mind, it is very easy to build rapport with the audience.

TELLING STORIES

In previous sections I explained the importance of using story and metaphor to deliver ideas. No place is it more important than it is here. People learn through stories. It is how we're programmed from early childhood. Whether you're selling widgets or explaining quantum physics, metaphors provide understanding. If the listener understands the benefits of what you offer, they're more likely to listen, buy, or participate. Using a metaphor is like tuning a radio to a specific station- it gives the listener something they can hear clearly.

One important distinction when using metaphors in presentations versus coaching is in regards to clarity. Usually with therapeutic metaphors, the meaning is specific to the individual. It is built on their model of the world, rather than that of the general population. But when using metaphors in group presentations, it is best to use references that a majority of your listeners will easily understand. You may have noticed that I have used many examples throughout this book drawn from popular culture, like current TV shows and movies. They may not work for everyone, but the chances are much higher using pop culture than obscure philosophical references (unless, of course, your audience is a group of philosophers).

USE HUMOR APPROPRIATELY

Yes, I know, this idea scares most people. You've probably attended some lecture or seminar and the leader told really bad jokes. Don't worry – I'm not going to suggest telling jokes at all. This tactic works for some people, but not everyone. What I mean by humor is the ability to make people laugh or chuckle. Telling stupid or offensive jokes usually breaks rapport and is best left out of a presentation.

Humor can be defined as the mental faculty of discovering, expressing, or appreciating the ludicrous or absurdly incongruous. When determining whether or not to use humor, first calibrate your audience. Do you have enough rapport, and are they ready to have fun? If they are in a sour mood, you may need to pace and lead for a while before trying to be funny. Being aware of your audience is key to being a successful presenter.

The basics of humor are simple. First, use ambiguity. Second, use as few words as possible to make an impact. Third, use your voice to convey meaning.

USING AMBIGUITY

Why is the man (or woman) who invests all your money called a broker?
George Carlin

In Part 6, I covered the use of ambiguity in Covert Hypnosis. Understand that ambiguity is also the root of humor. Because the English language is full of ambiguity, it is very easy to mistake one meaning for another.

Groucho Marx's classic joke depends on a grammatical ambiguity for its humor. For example, *"Last night I shot an elephant in my pajamas.*

What he was doing in my pajamas I'll never know." Every time I see a sign that reads, "Parking in rear," I chuckle a little.

Often, humor and humility can be combined very effectively. Telling humorous stories about yourself, or using your own personal failings to demonstrate some point you are trying to make, can be both entertaining and illuminating.

USE FEWER WORDS

I have listened to enough stories, metaphors, and anecdotes in my life to know the one thing that turns people off is the use of too many words. If you've ever watched the deleted scenes from a movie, you can clearly see why they were deleted. Any extraneous information needs to be removed to generate the greatest emotional impact. And whether you're selling widgets or books, people buy based on emotional arousal.

Now, I don't tend to fully script my lectures. However, I always have an objective in mind, and I allow the audience to direct the stories and metaphors I use. But you should know that I have a mental warehouse full of metaphors I have developed over many years, and I have practiced telling them in a variety of situations. I've calibrated my audience and found how best to tell each one so that now all I need to do is deliver them. If you are just starting out, write them down, work them out, and delete any unnecessary details.

Once you've written your presentation and metaphors using as few words as possible, take some time to determine where to put your emphasis.

TONALITY AND EMPHASIS

I'm not concerned about all hell breaking loose, but that a PART of hell will break loose...it'll be much harder to detect.
George Carlin

One secret to using humor is to use tone, inflection, and emphasis when speaking. Just as a magician uses misdirection, you can use your voice to convey meaning. George Carlin was a master of using his voice to get his audience laughing. Watch some of his stand up routines from the late 1970's and you'll know what I mean.

By now, you already know how important tonality is to conveying meaning. If you're trying to make a sale and your voice comes across as incongruent, your customer will hear it. However, it is incongruence that makes things funny. But what about the importance of emphasis? Consider the following sentence with the emphasis placed on different words.

"I would like to GO to dinner with you (rather than stay home)."
"I WOULD like to go to dinner with you (but I'm not going to)."
"I would like to go to dinner with YOU (as opposed to someone else)."

Do you hear the difference in meaning that comes from emphasizing the different words? If you're not careful, you can miscommunicate quite easily. So, make sure your tonality and inflection matches what you intend to convey.

Your Nonverbal Communication is Important

Developing the Appropriate Posture

You may remember from earlier chapters that your posture has a large effect on your emotional state and vice versa. If you want to achieve and maintain a great presenter state, you've got to use an appropriate posture. Specific postures also convey a message nonverbally. If you want your audience to respond positively to you, consider how you carry yourself.

Because I studied dance as a child, I learned quite a bit about creating good posture. What I found out is that certain postures look aggressive, others look weak, and some are elegant and poised. What type of posture do you think works best for you?

As a presenter, I find that it is usually best to come across as confident and humble. If you face your listeners head on with your chest puffed out, it may seem aggressive and confrontational, creating resistance in your audience. If you turn your back or slump your shoulders, you appear to be weak or nervous. A poised posture is centered and grounded, and faces the audience at a gentle angle. Imagine a shaft of light that's as strong as a steel bar that goes down through your body from the top of your head. It holds your body upright, your shoulders square, and your limbs and hips fluid. Think of a ballet dancer. Their bodies are elongated, and their feet are always at a slight angle.

Practicing a new posture is crucial, so that it seems natural when you give your presentations. It's not easy to retrain your physical presence overnight. It takes a little while to get your muscles relaxed into a new position. A fresh posture will feel weird at first, so practice holding it in front of a mirror. This will ensure you're getting it right. And remember, you can always use a role model to develop your most appropriate stance.

USING YOUR VOICE FOR MAXIMUM EFFECTIVENESS

> **Try this at Home- Developing Your Voice**
> Practice speaking from different places. Put one finger on your nose, and say one sentence. Listen to how it sounds.
> Place one finger on your throat, chest, gut, and diaphragm. Repeat the sentence in each place. Decide which works best for your voice. You can test out its effectiveness by telling a story to some friends and calibrating their reaction.

One major mistake made by public speakers is speaking too softly. Of course, having a microphone greatly helps, but it's not fool proof. Speaking quietly is often perceived as nervousness, and you already know where that leads. It can also be frustrating to your audience, particularly if they have paid to hear you.

In order to be heard and come across as confident and intelligent, make sure to BREATHE. Not only will this make your voice louder, it will help give it more resonance. Why is resonance important? Sound affects matter, and a deep resonance can be very hypnotic and captivating. This may not always be your objective, but it will work most of the time. To create resonance, be sure to breathe deeply and speak from your diaphragm. A nasally voice is quite unpleasant, as you might guess.

Another important consideration is rhythm, especially if you want to give hypnotic and captivating performances. The first person who comes to mind here is Garrison Keillor. He once gave a performance sitting in a chair alone on stage, and throughout the entire hour tapped his foot rhythmically while speaking to that cadence. Talk about hypnotic! Nearly the entire audience began tapping with him, unconsciously. He had everyone entranced. If you want to become a master story-teller, listen and watch him in action!

GET YOUR AUDIENCE IN THE RIGHT STATE

Many individuals come in to a presentation with un-resourceful states, such as boredom, irritation, or insecurity. These states are detrimental to your presentation, and getting through them should be your first priority. Remember to pace their experience before leading them into new states. You can pace the group by acknowledging their feelings using language and by building rapport nonverbally.

Your audience will go into the state you are in, especially if you have rapport. Therefore, the first secret to leading them into the state you want them in is to go into it yourself. If you want your group to have fun, have fun yourself. If you want them to be in a buying mood, get yourself into a hungry state. If you want them curious, lift your eyebrows.

Personally, I like active participation at my seminars. I get my audience's bodies involved as much as possible. I have them stand and stretch, introduce themselves to their neighbor, and have them do short practice exercises with other participants. Not only does this solidify their learning into their bodies, it promotes a friendly and active environment. Consider what type of mood you want to set.

Be sure to set the stage. When I was younger, my family belonged to a church. I really didn't like going at all. I realized years later that, to me, celebrating faith is more romantic than practical. Our church looked like a school auditorium. The walls were white, the carpet blue, and the chairs looked like they belonged in a hotel. It didn't fit my ideal, so I often tuned out. Of course, the venue isn't always in your control, but you can add elements that will target your audience. You can affect the look and feel of slide presentations, select the right music and lighting, or captivate your audience with your words. In any case, set the stage as much as possible.

ANCHORING LISTENERS

Once you've led your audience into an appropriate state, there are three main ways to anchor that state in your audience; spatially, auditorily, and visually.

Spatial anchors link mental and emotional states to specific locations in space, like spots on a stage, or a chair or podium. Some people even walk off the stage into the audience and use places there. To set this type of anchor, get your listeners into the state you desire while you stand in a specific place. Then, any time you want to trigger the state, move back into that place. Remember to only use that spot for triggering your desired state. Spatial anchors are best employed when you have a stage or a fair amount of space in front of a room.

If you're speaking in a board room, you may prefer to use visual anchors. My favorite type of visual anchor is gesture. Gestures not only can be used to anchor new states, there are many that have already been anchored. Some gestures even generate states. I know one speaker that puts his hand up in a stop position and shakes his head every time the audience laughs. Then, when he wants to elicit a laugh, he makes the motion again. It works every time.

Some other options for visual anchors are pointing to specific objects or products. If you can link good feelings to your products, you're going to increase sales. Some trainers use stuffed animals as anchors and link learning states to them, which also adds a measure of playfulness to the class. To set visual anchors, elicit the state you wish to anchor, and then introduce the visual cue.

> **Example of Looped Story**
> A few years ago, I was riding on the handlebars of my old boyfriend's bike. We hit a bump in the road, and I fell down and hurt my knee. I know you have all had an experience of getting hurt by someone you care for. When it happened to me, I said to myself, know more Mr. Nice Guys.
> You know, you thought you had to break into (in 2) a new awareness of yourself. My best friend's little girl just realized she has fingers and toes. She looks at herself and...
> Long Pause
> You're probably wondering, and it's useful to wonder, how to learn from your past that point where healing takes place now.
> Just like it did for me in Brazil. I went to see this spiritual healer and...
> You know, understanding is on the way to healing. Like it when you have the opportunity to bring your issues to lighten up.
> The spiritual healer allowed me to heal myself. And what I was going to say earlier is that my friend's little girl is beginning to realize who she is. I got back up off the ground, brushed myself off, and move on.

Auditory anchors are generally easy to employ, and they can be used in almost every situation. If every time you encounter a limiting belief or block from someone you smile and ask, "Is that the truth?" you'll anchor your listeners to calling their limitations into question in a gentle and fun way. There are several universal sounds that can be used, or you can generate new ones. I often tell my classes a story about an adventure I had in Belize a few years ago, and in it I hum the theme song from Indiana Jones as a resource for overcoming fearful situations. Then, when I encounter a student with a strong fear I use the song again, and they almost always begin to laugh.

Regardless of which type of anchoring you choose to employ, think it out before you get in front of your group. Practice it several times until it begins to feel natural.

Using Nested Loops to Chain States

One of the most interesting methods for keeping your listeners engaged is to use open and nested loops. This method for using metaphors and stories can be used to chain your audience through a variety of emotional states, or it can be used to create amnesia for delivering embedded commands, which you will remember from Part 5. Looping metaphors also generates curiosity and promotes attention.

One of my favorite comedians of all times is Robin Williams. In his stand up routines he picks a theme, and all of his bits come back to the theme at some point, even when all the stories have completely different content. This method of storytelling is also employed by a variety of comedians, screen writers, and authors. It's not very interesting to tell one story all the way through, but if you tell one part then talk about something else for a while and come back to the story later, the whole time you're off topic your audience will be on the edge of their seats waiting for the conclusion.

By now you've probably figured out that nested loops are stories strategically embedded in a talk. To effectively and easily use looped stories, you will want to plan out your talk in advance. Make an outline of your talk, including your introduction, main points, and conclusion. Then, decide what emotional states your audience is likely to come in the door with, how you want them to feel during your presentation, and how you want them to feel when they leave. Consider what stories or metaphors will elicit those states. You'll probably want at least five stories; one or two for the introduction, two or three for the actual presentation, and another one or two for the conclusion.

One format that is best used for lectures and sales presentations is as follows:

First part of introduction story 1 → First part of introduction story 2 → Some Content → First part of story 3 → First part of story 4 → Full Story 5 →

Finish story 4 → Finish story 3 → Finish story 2 → Finish story 1 → Conclusion

Get the idea? The point is to tell only a portion of the story so that the audience is waiting for the conclusion. For the best results, tell the story to the point of most interest. Then move on to another story. Some stories can eventually be told to their completion; some can even be left unresolved. They don't even have to be finished in the same order in which they were told. You've got a lot of room to be creative.

One important thing to remember is that if you use a series of open loops, the nested story (the one embedded in the middle and told in its entirety) is likely going to be consciously forgotten. If you are presenting information that you need your listeners to remember, only use the stories to lead them into the state you want them in before presenting your content. Make them short and to the point. This will ensure that your listeners are in the best state possible to receive your information.

An alternative way to use looped stories is to intentionally create an amnesic state so that you can embed hypnotic suggestions. This format is best used for teaching information you want to impart to the unconscious mind. This is the style I most often employ in classes and private sessions. In this case, generate at least five stories, and place the embedded suggestions in the fifth story.

First part of story 1 → First part of story 2 → First part of story 3 → First part of story 4 → Full Story 5

Second part of story 4 → Second part of story 3 → Second part of story 2 → Second part of story 1

Practice using both formats, and find out which works best for your presentations. Remember that the main objective in using these stories is to lead your audience into the desired state for receiving your information. The stories or metaphors should evoke the state, rather than describe it. Keep in mind that humor is a great addition!

To build your stories, refer back to the section on metaphors. You can also use personal stories about funny things that happened getting to the venue, how you benefited from the information you're about to present, and inspirational experiences.

CHAPTER 28:
CONVEYING YOUR MESSAGE

In order to convey your intended message your language needs to be impeccable. There are some things you could say, or not say, that would hinder your message being received in the best way. Luckily, I've distilled a variety of useful tools for you in this chapter for easy incorporation into your presentations.

META PROGRAMS

You will probably remember that strategies are comprised of a series of internal representations, triggered by internal and external experiences. In the early days of NLP it was believed that if you installed someone else's strategy in its entirety, you would get the same results. Yet, Richard Bandler and Leslie Cameron-Bandler noticed that two people using the same strategy could get completely different results.

For example, two people that have the same strategy for spelling (Vr -> K) can have different responses. One might see the words (Vr = visual remembered) and feel certain (K = kinesthetic) they can spell it correctly. However, a second individual may see the words and feel uncertain of their ability to spell them. This is relevant to the process versus content debate mentioned in Part 6.

The notion of Meta Programs arose from attempting to discover what made the difference between such diverse responses. Because the general representational structure of the strategies was essentially the same, it was postulated that the differences came from patterns outside of, or 'meta to,' the strategy (or internal program); i.e., a 'Meta Program.'"

-- Dilts & DeLozier, Encyclopedia of Systemic Neuro-Linguistic Programming and NLP New Coding, 2000.

In her clinical practice, Leslie Cameron-Bandler, now Leslie LeBeau, identified 60 different meta programs. In conjunction with David Gordon, Robert Dilts, and Judith DeLozier, these programs were categorized and explained in depth. Since that time one of Leslie's students, Rodger Bailey, created the LAB profile, an application of Meta Programs for business popularized by Shelle Rose Charvet in her book, *Words That Change Minds.*

The majority of the **Meta Programs** I consider important will be covered in the next section of this volume. However, there are a few programs that influence your success when speaking to groups, such as:

- Motivation Direction

- Motivation Reason

- Motivation Source

- Decision Factors

- Working Scope

Meta Programs are important to understand, because they play a role in how your message is received. Since each individual has their own model of the world, the way in which you present information will determine how each individual responds. But, there are only a few distinctions you need to know to increase your ability to direct an individual's or group's behavior.

Using Meta Programs in your life and work is quite simple. When communicating to an individual, you first need to determine their particular program. Then you can use language that is appropriate to that program. Incorporating Meta Programs into group presentations is even easier. All that is required is to include language from each program distinction, so that each individual's program is addressed.

MOTIVATION DIRECTION

In most presentations you are seeking to generate motivation, whether it's to sell a book or product, to get people working together, or to inspire individuals to make a change. In any event, there are two distinct attitudes individuals take when motivating themselves.

Towards motivated individuals focus on the goal or the end result of a task or project. With these individuals, telling them what they're going to walk away with at the end of your talk will speak directly to their unconscious minds. They don't want to solve problems; they want to attain results.

Away motivated people act just the opposite. These folks are motivated to get away from pain or problems. They love to find solutions, regardless of the end result. Away motivators have difficulty staying on task when all they have is an outcome on which to focus. They would much rather be given challenges to overcome.

When you're working with groups, you don't always have the luxury of determining each participant's programming. Therefore, you'll have to mix in a little of each pattern in order to address everyone's motivation direction. How do you do this? It's simple: you speak their language.

Here is what I intend to cover during this lecture today (towards). *You're going to identify and discover how to attain the goals you have for yourself* (towards). *You'll get rid of the obstacles in your path and find out how to steer clear of potential failures* (away from). *What I'm not going to do is bore you with long-winded explanations* (away from).

MOTIVATION REASON

I learned the importance of addressing a person's motivation reason when I worked at a nonprofit organization in Washington state years ago. I came in to do a job, and after just a few weeks had made a list of everything I wanted to do differently. I found ways to streamline some processes that made me much more efficient. However, the receptionist, who had been working there nearly a decade, was quite upset. She told me, "We've been doing things this way for a long time, and they work just fine!" I realized then that my optional nature was clashing with her procedural preference.

People with an **Options** pattern are motivated by endless possibilities and new ways of doing things. They believe success is a matter of finding new solutions. They consistently develop new procedures that Procedural individuals follow.

Individuals with a **Procedures** pattern follow the steps others have laid out for them. They believe it is the procedure that leads to results, and any change in a procedure can and will lead to disaster.

Because I'm an options sorter, I'll give you two ways to address both patterns in a presentation. One technique is to weave in language that appeals to both types (as in the example below). The other option is to give the audience a procedure to follow, and then give an optional step or variation in the procedure.

First (procedures), *you'll have the opportunity* (options) *to identify and discover how to attain the goals you have for yourself. Then* (procedures), *you'll get rid of the obstacles in your path and find out how to steer clear of potential failures. What I'm not going to do is limit your choices in how to get results* (options).

MOTIVATION SOURCE

Some individuals make decisions based on their own knowledge and feelings, and others base their judgments on external factors, like a friend's recommendation or an audience's applause. **Internal** motivators are motivated to act on what's true for them, while **External** motivators need feedback to move forward. By addressing both styles, you'll be able to answer questions from your audience with more grace – and you'll be able to motivate them to buy your product or service much more easily.

In 2005 Hurricane Wilma ripped through south Florida, closing down most of the Atlantic Coast, including the hotel in which I was about to host an NLP training. I received numerous calls from participants around the country asking if it was safe to attend. Most were satisfied when I let them know I had found a new venue that had meeting space, sleeping rooms, and running water and electricity. One however, was not convinced. I listened to her concerns, but she responded with, "I'm just not sure I should come." So, I replied, "Well, only you will know if this is right for you at this time." She made it to class.

This process has worked for millions (external), *and you'll have a chance to find out for yourself how powerful it really is* (internal).

DECISION FACTORS

How would you change your presentation if you found out that 80% of people are scared of making a big change more than every couple of years? Imagine trying to sell a new computer to a customer every year. While it's certainly not impossible, it's highly unlikely. You could, however, sell them an upgrade every year or two.

Only about 20% of the population is comfortable making a major change every year or two. These individuals have a **Difference** factor. **Sameness** people comprise about 5% of the population, and they won't be OK with change but once every twenty years! The other 75% of individuals will consider upgrades, improvements, and evolutions every three to five years.

Now, I'm not suggesting you abandon launching a revolutionary new way to do business. I'm merely mentioning that it's important to; 1) determine your market, and 2) use the appropriate language for that market. Have you ever wondered why home improvement is such a trend? Most individuals are very comfortable with that term, even though the process is actually a major change. Cell phone companies know this too. They don't put out advertisements for buying a new phone; they suggest you upgrade your plan or phone. If you've fallen prey to those ads, you've got a **Sameness with Exception** factor.

When you're presenting to groups, it's best to use a variety of terms. You can call your product revolutionary, but then show how it's an improvement over an older design. Imply that they'll be able to do the same things they used to do without falling behind the times.

The material we're going to cover today is completely new, unique, and revolutionary (difference). *But don't worry; you'll recognize the similarities* (sameness) *to the system you already use. We'll use the same terms* (sameness) *and basic formula, but it's a great improvement over the old system* (sameness with exception).

WORKING SCOPE

Have you ever brought home a new game and tried to learn how to play it with someone? Most games come with detailed instructions and an objective, detailing how to play and how to win. A person that usually reads the objective first is often frustrated and confused if someone reads them the rules first instead. Of course, the reverse is also true – the person that likes to read the rules first will quickly become confused if only given the objective. This is the difference between a Specific and General working scope.

A person with a **Specific** scope is very detail oriented, and they often speak in sequences. A person with a **General** scope focuses more on the big picture. They don't much care for details, except when learning something new. In conversation, a person with a general scope will be wondering when the specific person will get to the point, and the specific individual will tend to mistrust the general individual. Can you tell my pattern by this paragraph?

In any presentation, you want to include both the specifics and the objective. Before explaining an NLP process to a class, I usually begin with the main idea I want to convey. Then I give the detailed instructions. I finish up by stating the objective again. This ensures that everyone feels comfortable with the process, partially due to the fact that about 60% of the population has a general scope.

The main objective (general) is to set and achieve your important goals. And here is how precisely to do that (specific)... Essentially, if you set well formed goals, you're able to achieve them quickly and easily (general). Here are the exact criteria you need to satisfy (specific).

Now, let's put it all together. I hope it's not too general for you!

Here is what I intend to cover during this lecture today (towards). First (procedures), you'll have the opportunity (options) to identify and discover how to attain the goals you have for yourself (towards). Then (procedures), you'll get rid of the obstacles in your path and find out how to steer clear of potential failures (away from). What I'm not going to do is bore you with long-winded explanations (away from) or limit your choices in how to get results (options). This process has worked for millions (external), and you'll have a chance to find out for yourself how powerful it really is (<u>internal</u>). *The material we're going to cover today is completely new, unique, and revolutionary* (<u>difference</u>). *But don't worry, you'll recognize the similarities* (<u>sameness</u>) *to the system you already use. We'll use the same terms* (<u>sameness</u>) *and basic formula, but it's a great improvement over the old system* (<u>sameness with exception</u>). *The main objective* (<u>general</u>) *is to set and achieve your important goals. And here is how to do precisely that...* (<u>specific</u>).

REFRAMING PATTERNS

When giving presentations, you may be required to handle your audience's objections and limiting beliefs. This is a big concern when you're working with smaller, interactive groups. You might come upon objections like "it's too expensive" or "I don't want to be here." In these cases, the ability to reframe their thoughts and feelings is the key to managing the audience.

As mentioned earlier, there are two forms of limiting beliefs; **complex equivalence** and **cause and effect**. A complex equivalence attributes meaning to an experience, as in "It's too expensive (which means I can't afford it)." With the right reframe these beliefs are easy to shift. To do that you need to challenge the interpretation the individual made about their experience. In this case, the fact that something is expensive doesn't automatically mean it's unaffordable. A cause and effect belief links a predictable response to an experience, as in "Your talk upset me." For these beliefs, just challenge the link between the cause and the effect. With pure logic and reason it's easy to conclude that it wasn't the talk that was upsetting, especially if the rest of the audience enjoyed it. There must have been something inside that individual that allowed them to feel upset.

Mastering the following reframing patterns is an incredibly powerful skill, for your presentations and in your life. Once you've fully integrated these patterns into your life you'll have the ability to reframe any of your own "negative" experiences, which inevitably leads to more happiness and success. Consider two individuals having the same external experience of being in an accident. One person could emerge with the attitude of being glad to have survived. The other might survive, but with a sense of fear and anger at nearly being killed. These two different responses to the same experience indicate that reality is subjective. So if you're going to draw conclusions, they might as well lean towards the positive.

> **Try this at Home**
> Make a list of 3-4 common objections or limiting beliefs that surface in your listeners.
> Then, write a reframe for each one using every pattern listed below. Some will work well, and others won't. Cut the ones that don't, and practice delivering the ones that do.
> Optional: List some of your own limiting beliefs, and reframe them.
> If you do enough of these, you'll learn the patterns quite easily.

Reframing is useful in many areas of your life and work. I commonly use them in private sessions to reframe my client's limiting beliefs. I've used them to challenge the assumption that being overweight is genetic, that quitting smoking is hard, and that phobias are challenging to overcome. I think of these patterns as a way to question our programming. As you know, our beliefs come from our past experiences, our family, culture, and the media. It's very useful to challenge this programming, particularly when it's posing a challenge or keeping you from doing something you want to be able to do.

The following patterns, modeled by Robert Dilts, are all ways in which you can reframe limiting beliefs and challenge objections. Not every pattern will work for every limitation, so I recommend learning them all. If you understand that the intent is to change someone's obstacles, you'll keep trying different patterns until you find one that works. This takes practice, but it's not difficult to do.

Because reframing can come across as argumentative, it's imperative that these patterns be used after establishing rapport. I can't stress this point enough. If you use them without tact and rapport, you run the risk of upsetting your listeners. In the therapeutic context, it's very easy to get away with these, because the client is paying you to help them change. However, in a group setting they can be perceived as confrontational and rude. So, make sure your tone of voice conveys compassion and understanding, and ensure the rapport is firmly in place. You can always preface your responses with, "I'm curious…" or "I'm interested to know…" to help soften the reframe.

INTENT

With this pattern, you focus on the speaker's intention in stating the objection. This can be done by highlighting their positive intent behind the belief, or by challenging the negative intent. To highlight the positive intent in the belief, "I'm not capable of starting my own practice," ask, "What do you hope to gain by mentioning that?" Then you can use their answer to begin working out a solution.

You could also address the same objection by replying, "Is it important to you to have support in order to take on the challenge?" This statement assumes they are stating the objection in order to get your help. If you get their intent incorrect, though, this pattern could backfire.

CONSEQUENCE

With this pattern, your task is to find an unintended consequence in continuing to hold the belief being challenged. I like to think about what will happen if they continue to think in the same way. I really like this pattern, because it tends to open the discussion, giving you a chance to move forward creating a solution.

So, if a potential customer tells you that they don't need a new service provider because they already have one they are satisfied with, you may want to reply, "What's the likely outcome if you don't continually employ changes that will positively affect your company?" By indicating there is a potentially negative consequence to holding their position, you increase the likelihood of making a sale.

ANOTHER OUTCOME

This is the best pattern to know if you're giving interviews. Most politicians have this tool so well ingrained that when they are asked a question they don't want to deal with they shift to another outcome and start discussing their preferred topic. It's a very effective technique.

If you come up against the limitation, "I can't afford your package," you can reply, "The real issue here isn't about money, it's about finding the best solution for your business's particular needs." For the objection,

"We're not hiring right now," you could respond with, "Isn't it important to have the talent you need to take your business to the next level?"

Counter Example

Hands down my favorite reframing pattern, a counter example is a way to prove that the belief is not a fact. A counter example can be directed towards a particular outcome, or it can be used as a question that leads the listener to their own answer. This makes it easy to apply to almost any limitation.

To use this pattern, ask yourself, "When did A not equal B?" For the belief, "I can't get the time off work to attend," reply with, "You take time off work for other types of self-care, don't you?" You could also use a counter example from your own life, as in, "I used to think I couldn't take time off work, but then I realized that this seminar would improve my performance at work."

Apply to Self

Probably the most confrontational way to reframe a thought, this pattern can be extremely effective for dealing with hecklers. Use it with caution, though, as the common response to this technique is, "Ouch!"

The intention of this pattern is to point out how the individual's comment reflects their own limitation. For example, "I can't afford this," could be met with, "That's a costly assumption." The objection, "I don't have the time," could be reframed by saying, "Could you make the time?"

Reality Strategy

As I mentioned previously, many of our beliefs are programmed into us by people and the media. The tendency is to hold on to those beliefs, even if they aren't useful. By using the reality strategy, you're asking the listener to recognize where their belief came from, which gives them the opportunity to change their mind.

For example, if someone tells you that they can't figure out how to use your system you can responds with, "How do you know you can't figure it out?" They may respond with another limitation, such as, "I'm not smart enough," or, "Your manual is confusing." You can reply with another reality strategy, "What makes you think you're not smart enough?" or, "How would you know if that wasn't true?" The latter question is a great one to ask, because while the listener is considering how they would know they begin to imagine it differently. I consider it a magical question!

MODEL OF THE WORLD

This is one of the easiest patterns to learn. All you need to do is point out that what is true for your listener is not necessarily true for everyone. For example, if someone objects to your ideas by saying, "You can't do that," you can respond with a counter example like, "Mister X did something just as crazy last week, and it worked out great." You could also ask, "Don't you know anyone that has achieved what was once thought to be impossible?"

META FRAME

This patterns challenge the basis behind the belief, rather than the belief itself. This one works best for complex equivalences, such as, "I can't afford your service." This belief implies that the person doesn't expect the service to pay for itself.

To reframe a limiting belief using the Meta Frame, look for an additional belief that is implied by the limitation. You may respond, "Is it possible you assume that my service is going to cost more than it will make you?" It can also work for beliefs, such as "Your book was offensive," where the underlying assumption is that discussing certain topics or using certain words is wrong. A potential reply is, "Are you under the assumption that it's not OK to address taboo topics in order to prevent potential problems?"

HIERARCHY OF CRITERIA

Criteria are aligned hierarchically, and any given belief is aligned with a particular criterion. By considering what higher level of criteria your listener may be ignoring in their assumption, you can get an individual to shift their focus. To do this, you'll have to get an idea of what is important to them, so rapport building is going to be critical. This pattern is also very easy to use, because your response will usually begin with, "Isn't it more important to...?"

If you were giving a sales presentation, and a potential customer offered the objection, "I've already got a good system in place, and I don't really need another one," you could reply with, "Isn't it more important that you stay on the cutting edge to compete in today's market?" In this case, staying on the cutting edge is assumed to be the relevant higher criteria.

CHANGE FRAME SIZE

Changing the frame size of a limiting belief is the classic reframing pattern. With this pattern, you're either exaggerating the belief (making it bigger) or breaking it down into something more specific (making it smaller).

Let's assume that someone holds the belief that they can't get out of bed on time. You can either exaggerate the belief by replying, "Are you physically incapable of arising earlier?" or reduce frame size by responding with, "When was the last time you did get up on time?"

For the limitation, "I've read about NLP, but I don't think I need live training," you may respond with, "Honestly, it's the difference between reading about football and playing football."

CHUNK DOWN

You may remember chunking down from the Meta Model. When you chunk down, you get more specific information. This is often helpful, because it challenges the actual assumption being made. This is also a very simple pattern to employ, as it is flexible enough to be used for a majority of assumptions and objections. Just as in the Meta Model, this pattern will provide you with more information from the person you're communicating with. This can open the dialogue and get you to a solution much more quickly.

For the belief, "I can't afford it," reply with "How, specifically, do you know you can't afford it?" or "What, specifically, about it can't you afford?" For the assumption, "I'm not ready to be a public speaker," reply with, "How specifically will you know when you are ready?"

CHUNK UP

With this pattern you will exaggerate the limiting belief, making it seem ridiculous. It's very effective for some beliefs, but it won't necessarily work for everything. As with the Chunk Down pattern, this type of reframing results in further discussion. It isn't a zinger like the Apply to Self pattern, so be prepared to start a dialogue.

For fun, let's use the same beliefs from the previous example. For the belief, "I can't afford it," reply with, "There's absolutely no possible way you can scrape together the money?" or, "What's important about believing that?" For the assumption, "I'm not ready to be a public speaker," you could reply with, "Are you saying that you don't have the ability to speak outside of your bedroom?"

METAPHOR/ANALOGY

By this point you know how much I enjoy using metaphors. Another application of this tool is to reframe a limiting belief, because a metaphor can present a totally different way of thinking about something. If you can develop a metaphor that fits in with your listeners' experience, it will be even more effective.

If you come up against the objection that someone doesn't need to switch to your product or service because it's easier to stay with their current system, you may wish to offer an analogy. Try, "There was a time when people resisted switching to recycling, but now we know how important it is." Or, "You wouldn't leave your radio tuned to static, would you?"

If someone said to you, "We're not hiring," you might respond with, "I used to play sports in school, and the most successful teams were the ones that were able to spot and recruit great talent." For the assumption, "I'm not ready to be a public speaker," reply with, "Does the clock have to be ready to get plugged in?"

REDEFINE

Beliefs are actually decisions that were made as a result of a particular experience. Complex equivalences are created by attributing meaning to that experience. For these types of beliefs, redefining that meaning is incredibly helpful. For that reason, this is one of my most favorite patterns. A useful structure for this is the formula, "A does not = B, A = C, and that's D."

Consider the belief, "No one wants to hear me talk; I have nothing valuable to say." A good redefine would be, "It's not that you have nothing to say (A is not B), it's that you don't have confidence in yourself (A=C), and that's possible to change right now (D)."

For the belief, "Buying your product means paying a significant up-front cost." Redefine the belief with, "Buying it does not mean a high up-front cost it means you're making a great investment in your future, and that's critical in this economy."

Now that you know the patterns, come up with several reframes for objections you often receive in your work, in your relationships, or in yourself. Practice using them whenever possible to determine which ones work the best in your life and work.

MORE CONSIDERATIONS ABOUT PRESENTATIONS

By this point you have a lot of tools to make your presentations interesting and memorable. There are just a few more topics to cover to make you an excellent presenter.

UTILIZATION

When giving presentations, you can't control everything. So, it's useful to remember to employ Utilization. I've found that most of the "negative" things that happen when I'm speaking can be handled by keeping this principle in mind: everything that happens can be used to my advantage.

If people get up and start to head for the door, I can stop what I'm doing and ask for feedback. Was there something about my topic, my style, or my manner of presentation that was offensive to them? Were they simply in the wrong room at the start and didn't know it? Even if everyone walked out and refused to give me a reason, I could ultimately find ways to benefit from this experience. At the very least, I could use it as the opening for my next presentation. "You know, I gave this same talk the other day and everyone in the audience walked out in the first ten minutes. That's my current record, so I guess we'll just have to see what happens today."

The same principle holds for dealing with hecklers or people who ask harsh or confrontational questions. If you assume that nothing truly bad can ever happen when you're speaking in public, you'll be amazed how well you can relate to such events and how often you can indeed use them to your advantage. Johnny Carson is a good role model for developing this skill. No matter how his audience responded Carson was always ready to use their response, positive or negative, to make another joke.

KEEP IT SIMPLE

Too many aspiring presenters assume that to give a great presentation they have to pack it with information. I found this out the hard way.

I once gave a lecture to a group of spiritually hungry individuals. It was a large group of folks, and I really wanted to do well. So, I put together a talk that covered principles from everything I had ever studied on the subject. I packed what I had learned over ten years into a four-hour workshop. Talk about bad planning! Everyone in the room was overwhelmed by the breadth and depth I had covered. They were intrigued, but because I had given them too much to process in that short time they left not remembering anything.

The lesson? Keep it simple! Pick just a few points you want to make and go in depth on them. The majority of your audience will not have your level of understanding, so make it very easy for them to get what you're saying- even if it seems over simplified for you. They will appreciate it, and they will thank you.

MANAGE THE ENERGY OF THE ROOM

Great presenters have the ability to "read a room." They can easily calibrate the energy level of the audience, as well as individuals in the audience. Using your calibration skills, you'll be able to read others as well. If your group starts zoning out and finding other things to do rather than listen to you, change your approach. Get yourself into a better state and pull them back in using a personal story. If they are too anxious or too high energy, speak in a down tempo, and take them into a light trance.

This particular consideration also involves the age of your group. Adults can usually stay present for an hour or so. For that reason, I give short recesses every hour to keep everyone's energy up. Children, however, have much shorter attention spans. They need to shift every fifteen to thirty minutes in order to maintain focus. I find the easiest way to maintain attention is to give your audience an activity or exercise to do, even if it only takes five minutes. This keeps them actively involved in the process.

In short, use your calibration skills to read the audience, and make sure they stay in the state in which you want them.

SUMMARY

Presentations are tons of fun, incredibly rewarding, and they open you to endless possibilities. Improving your ability to speak in public is valuable to everyone. You present yourself in job interviews, meeting prospects, and when teaching others. Once you develop your ability to incorporate the tools below, you're on your way to giving great presentations.

- Use specific gestures and postures to increase you` impact and flexibility.

- Communicate confidence and authority.

- Direct your audience's state of mind consistently.

- Handle difficult audiences and hecklers by utilizing their behavior to your advantage.

- Entertain your audience using humor appropriately.

- Use metaphors, anecdotes and analogies to really put your message across.

- Maintain and manage the energy in the room.

- Be charismatic by speaking in loops and telling great stories.

STUDY QUESTIONS

1. What are the 5 main qualities of great presenters?
2. How can you become charismatic?
3. What types of humor are appropriate to use in a group?
4. How do you generate emotional states in an audience?
5. Which Meta Programs, Sleight of Mouth patterns, and Magic Word can you incorporate into your presentations to heighten your success?

PART 8:
SUCCESS SKILLS

SUCCESS SKILLS-
MODELING AND GENERATING PEAK
STATES

One of the cornerstones of NLP is the belief that failure is not really failure, but feedback that can be used to generate future success. I've learned more from my supposed failures than I have from my apparent successes. When you take time to evaluate your so-called failures, you have the opportunity to learn many things. A classic example is Thomas Edison, who made 1,000 attempts to create the light bulb. When asked about his progress, he claimed to have found 999 ways not to make a light bulb. Talk about perseverance!

After we had conducted thousands of experiments on a certain project without solving the problem, one of my associates, after we had conducted the crowning experiment and it had proved a failure, expressed discouragement and disgust over our having failed to find out anything. I cheerily assured him that we had learned something. For we had learned for a certainty that the thing couldn't be done that way, and that we would have to try some other way.
Thomas Edison

Experience, by its very nature, provides us an opportunity to gain wisdom. It is our experience that fashions our beliefs and ideas of the world. To be truly successful in every area of our lives, it's imperative the interpretations and meanings we derive from those experiences be productive and sustainable. If our judgments are inappropriate, we find ourselves limited in our thinking and in our actions. Flexibility is paramount to success.

There are a number of ways to become more flexible in your life and work. You can change your beliefs about what you can and can't do, you can shift how you feel in certain situations, and you can expand your identity to include a larger range of behaviors and feelings. In previous chapters I presented information on changing your feelings and beliefs, but in the following chapters I will give you the knowledge you need to broaden your identity. You'll learn about the logical levels and why your identity is so important. You'll also gain insight into modeling, which is where NLP began.

The ability to model yourself and others is a skill every master practitioner of NLP employs. **Modeling** is the ability to gather the relevant information about a particular skill from an individual that has that skill, and then apply that learning. If I wanted to be able to speak in public as easily and confidently as Oprah Winfrey, I would need to gather information from watching and listening to her show. Then, I would distill that information and practice using it until I was able to get the same results. Sounds great, right?

CHAPTER 29:
MODELING SUCCESS

NLP is probably best known for modeling. No surprise, since the ability to model another person in order to expand your skill set or gain understanding about someone else's map of the world is extremely useful in a variety of situations. The concept is simple, but doing it correctly can sometimes be time consuming.

Modeling is a natural process. Every human being learns it as a child. We naturally model the individuals in our environment, picking up their habits, beliefs, and values by watching and listening. Some of the things we have modeled have been useful, but others may cause problems. The only difference between the modeling we do as children and that which we do as resourceful adults is in our ability to evaluate behaviors, choosing what we want to model. When we are between the ages of eight to fourteen we don't always have a strong internal evaluating strategy. As adults we learn that there are certain things we don't want to model, and we can be much more discerning and intentional, rather than haphazard.

There are two main ways to use modeling; self modeling and modeling others. In self modeling, you elicit your own internal strategies and states that lead you to specific outcomes from which others may benefit. When modeling others, you elicit someone else's strategies and thought patterns so that you can benefit from their skills.

How to Use Modeling

Self Modeling

I had a student a few years back that ate sweets compulsively. She was very unhappy with her figure, but she just couldn't resist desserts. She asked me one day how I stayed thin. When I mentioned that I hardly ever eat sweets or snacks of any kind, she was very intrigued. I explained further that if I did have a craving for chocolate (the only sweet craving I ever have) I would eat two bites and feel satisfied. By this point, a few students had overheard, and so we began a modeling process.

What I determined was that I've always had the belief that sugar is very bad for me, because I'm at risk of diabetes. I stopped eating it altogether at age 12, and because I use Away Motivation, knowing I don't want diabetes is enough to get me to eat sugar sparingly. I also highly value staying in shape and feeling healthy. So, I developed a strategy that every time I want to eat something sweet, I smell it, take a bite, and savor it fully using my gustatory and kinesthetic senses. Then I feel satisfied. I know I'm satisfied because I say to myself, "That was really good," and by stating it in the past tense, I know I'm done.

After lunch that day, I brought in a bar of organic dark chocolate and gave everyone a piece the size I would normally eat. I ran them through every part of my model, and everyone was satisfied after their tiny pieces! Several of them have continued to use the model with great success. The way I took them through the model was to install the beliefs I have about sugar and led them through a process to push health higher on their hierarchy of values. Then, we installed the actual strategy I use, anchoring the state of satisfaction after eating the food.

Modeling Others

There are many reasons to model another individual. You may wish to learn a strategy that works in another field that will also apply to your own, as in modeling teamwork in an athletic club and using the model to enhance teamwork in your business. If you're a writer or actor, modeling is an excellent skill to have. Many characters are loosely based on real individuals, or a combination of attributions garnered from a variety of models. NLP practitioners use modeling in their change work to assist clients in successfully overcoming an issue that someone else has already transcended.

When modeling, it's important to select the right person and context, otherwise what you end up with may not be what you want. If, for example, you want to stop smoking, and you choose a role model who has never smoked, you'll learn how to never smoke. Conversely, if you model someone who used to smoke, you'll learn how to transition from your current state to your desired state.

In order to model others, you must understand all three **perceptual positions**. You may remember this from language classes in school. First position, like first person narration, is characterized by looking through your own eyes, fully associated in your own body. This position is used in anchoring, to produce strong internal feelings. Second position is the position of "other," where you're associated into another person's body, feeling their feelings, and living through their model of the world. This position is employed in deep trance identification and re-imprinting because it offers the option of living in someone else's world, which provides perspective. The third position, or meta position, is a dissociated state. It's the observer position, where you're watching yourself in relation to another person or situation. This position is used frequently in NLP to get distance from painful experiences and traumas, because the dissociation removes strong feelings. It's a great position to use for learning from experiences, as it's more objective than the other positions.

Logical Levels in Modeling

According to Robert Dilts and his work with Logical Levels, there is more to modeling than you may think. Every model that exists does so, not in a vacuum, but within a particular Environment. While the focus of most modeling is on the Capability level (the how), you can't ignore the Behaviors (the what), Beliefs (the why), and Identity (the who). Yet, the Capabilities of a model provide the leverage to create the resulting identity, values and beliefs as behaviors in a particular environment. For example, knowing how someone makes a hole-in-one can give you insights into how they think, who they believe themselves to be, and what they're likely to do in certain circumstances.

Modeling, as stated earlier, is more than eliciting an individual's strategy for doing a particular action. Capabilities are more than procedures; they are frequently "non-linear" in their application. If you think back to the T.O.T.E. model of strategies, there is a feedback loop that includes the goal and assessment of whether or not that goal has been achieved. It is more than a linear procedure. If you're eliciting a strategy for spelling, there is a built-in check for determining whether or not each individual word is spelled correctly (the test phase of the strategy). This is one reason eliciting strategies can be complicated – they aren't necessarily organized as "a, then b, then c." Typically, they follow more along the lines of this: decide to spell a word, imagine that word, and check if it feels right, and if it does, go ahead and spell it. If it doesn't feel right, then follow another procedure to get it right. The strategy starts off in a linear sequence, but at the test point, it can deviate toward a completely new direction.

So, when modeling, it's important to keep in mind that you want to start by eliciting the strategy the individual uses to do the behavior you wish to model. And remember, that strategy isn't a sequence of steps; it's got a variety of tracks that can spin off, depending on results, feelings, and the environment in which it's being used. A few more things you'll need to know are: the goals of the individual being modeled, how they gauge their progress, the behaviors they use to achieve their goals, and how the person responds if they don't achieve the goal.

A MODEL OF COMPASSION

Since this is a chapter on modeling, I'm going to present a model of someone I know that is extremely compassionate, tolerant, and understanding. While this model is not overly complex, it will serve to illustrate all of the aspects to eliciting, sorting through, and utilizing an existing model.

The woman I have chosen to model, we'll call her Alice, is very spiritually oriented, as you will see from her responses to my questions. It should be noted that when gathering information from an individual you're modeling, it is important to use their words and sensory information. Later, you will be able to weed out any extraneous pieces of the model. In Alice's case, I found she believed her ability to be compassionate was based on her faith in God, but I've modeled others with different beliefs who are also profoundly caring individuals. Whatever your personal convictions, it's a good idea as an NLP practitioner to get in the habit of accepting people's faith without passing judgment. At this stage, we're simply gathering information.

ENVIRONMENT

The environment level establishes when and where the skill is demonstrated by the role model, including when and where it isn't used. I asked Alice when she demonstrated compassion, and I got a very long list of contexts. So, I asked her when she didn't always demonstrate it, and she mentioned she had momentary slips of bickering with her spouse, but that it never lasted more than a few moments. There were no location restraints, but her ability to be understanding mostly surfaced when dealing with someone in trouble, which she defined as angry, upset, or experiencing their own failure.

BEHAVIOR

At the level of behavior, you determine what the person being modeled actually does when they're in the specific environment you have identified. When I asked Alice what she does when someone is in trouble, she recognized that her main tactic was to listen to them without judgment. She just lets the person talk as long as they need without interruption. Additionally, she may also provide support financially, emotionally, or physically. One thing she does every time, after the person is finished talking, is to provide advice based on her faith.

CAPABILITIES

Now, at this point we're determining the thinking process behind the behaviors we elicited. As previously mentioned, this is the level where most of the modeling work is done. Here we are discovering the mental strategies being used.

When I asked Alice to remember the last time she demonstrated compassion, she recounted to me an example of being asked for money by a drug addict in her immediate family. What I was able to distill from her story is that when someone comes to her in trouble, she listens to them completely, without interruption, except to clarify her understanding of their situation. She lets them complete their story and talk until they run out of steam. Then, she says, "I'm sorry that happened," "you poor thing," or "bless your heart." During the time she's listening, she's giving the person the benefit of the doubt, reserving judgment until after she has prayed about it. Yet, during the conversation, she will dispense advice and help the person find a solution to their dilemma.

When Alice intuits (K+ and A) that she needs to do something to help the person in need, she prays and reads the bible, opening randomly to any page for inspiration. If she is still uncertain, she meditates to regain her strength.

In the situation with the drug addict, she was unsure whether or not to help him financially. So, she asked him, "Do you realize you made a big mistake by using again?" When he said yes, she asked him to commit to making a change. Once he did so, they came up with a plan to get him out of debt. Here is Alice's strategy for giving someone another chance when they've made a mistake.

THE STRATEGY FOR COMPASSION AND HELPING

Alice's **Trigger** for going into compassion is finding out that someone she knows is in trouble, which usually comes in the form of being told (Ae) by the person in trouble. This external trigger leads to an internal response of empathy, which, for her, is a feeling of identifying with the person in trouble.

The **Operation** phase starts with her getting calm (K+). Then, Alice listens to the whole sequence of events (A), speaking only to clarify details. She asks leading questions with a inquisitive tonality like "Do you mean___?" Regardless of their answer, she replies with rapport by saying, "I thought so," or "I didn't think so," depending on their response. While she listens, she looks for the intent behind the mistakes (Vc) the individual has made. This is her first test to determine how she should respond.

If Alice feels the intent is good (K+), she then proceeds to help the person find a solution. She asks herself (Ad), "What can we do to resolve this?" If the intent is not to make a change, then she exits the scene without attempting to help.

Alice's second **Test** is whether or not the individual in trouble realizes they've made a mistake. Have they learned from the mistake, and are they committed to making a change? Her way of determining this is to check their communication for congruence, which she decides based on their tonality and her intuition (A and K+). She also asks herself (Ad) if what she can do is enough to fill the gap in their new plan. In other words, whether what she has to offer can actually help them to move forward. If so, she will help. If not, she'll give advice on how to get the help they need.

THE STRATEGY FOR DEALING WITH CONFLICT WITH COMPASSION

Because harmony is one of Alice's highest values, every time she is confronted by another person's anger or hostility, she seeks immediately to resolve the issue. Her other main Trigger for going into compassion is when someone is angry with her. She knows someone is angry by the tone of their voice (A).

The Operation phase of Alice's strategy is, when she feels a person's confusion and irritation, she asks herself, (Ad) "How do we fix this?" Then, she matches and mirrors the person, building rapport, and relies on her prior communication training by asking the person for clarification, backtracking, and by using an appropriate tone for that person. She has a variety of techniques she uses for resolution of the problem.

Alice's Tests assess whether the person is feeling calmer and whether her own needs are being met. If both criteria are met, she exits to another strategy. If they aren't, she'll try additional tactics involving being nice and understanding. Occasionally the strategy loops here, between her checking if the criteria are satisfied and trying more techniques to get her needs met. She doesn't exit until she has been successful, or until she's run out of communication techniques. If she doesn't exit successfully, she will release any remaining tension, deciding to deal with the person another day.

BELIEFS AND VALUES

The beliefs and values of a role model are often critical to their success. This is one of the first pieces of information I want to know about my models, because they form a framework in which the individual behaves.

In Alice's case, she believes with absolute certainty that God never gives anyone anything they can't handle. She knows that God has a purpose for everyone and that things will always get better, and that people are God's children and deserve love, support, and non-judgment. She also believes that everyone makes mistakes, and that since God and Jesus can forgive mistakes then she can as well.

Alice values harmony, and that value drives her belief that you have to pick your battles. She doesn't feel it's important to be right, only that it's important to get along and stay connected to others. Connection is another very high value for her, so all her actions are based on love and compassion. The third highest value I was able to elicit from her is joy. I believe that this leads her to seek resolution to conflict quickly, so that she can "feel God" more of the time.

IDENTITY

How a role model sees themselves is a good indication of their values and beliefs. I often determine a person's identity first, because it will help me understand their model of the world. A person's identity affects every aspect of their lives, particularly their behaviors, just like their beliefs and values, mostly because an identity is a belief about self.

Alice has several identities, as most individuals do, but I'm only concerned about the identity in relation to her ability to be compassionate. In this context, she sees herself as a child of God and a messenger of God's love. This identity drives her to lead by example.

SPIRITUAL

I think of the spiritual level as the mission or purpose that affects how an individual relates to the larger world. It is the highest motivator that drives how an individual operates on the earth. Information gathered on this level provides details about how the role model relates to family, society, culture, etc.

Again, an individual can have several missions in life, and they can change throughout life, but we're only concerned about the purpose within the stated context. For Alice, her big "why" is to be like Jesus. She has a strong desire to model him, which is probably evident from the information I've already provided.

I believe Alice is so successful at being compassionate, because there is no conflict between her beliefs, values, and actions. She wants to be an example of God's love by living as Jesus did, and she has developed strategies garnered from the Bible and from communication courses that assist her in doing so. Every thought and action is aligned with her mission in life. This is the hallmark of a successful model.

Implicit and Explicit Modeling

In my master practitioner trainings, I have students play a modeling game. One person closes their eyes, associates into a state of doing something they love, while the other students match their physiology. Then, they have to guess what the person they're modeling is doing, without words of any kind. It's an illuminating exercise, because most people are able to accurately guess.

This is called **implicit modeling**, and it involves acting like a role model and building intuitions about their inner state and thought process. It's very effective, because many people don't know what makes them successful, so asking them questions often leads to an "I don't know." Once people have mastered a skill, they no longer need to consciously remember how to do it. Implicit modeling overcomes this barrier.

Implicit modeling, then, is an intuitive process of understanding the other person's subjective experience by stepping into their shoes. By using this second perceptual position you can gain insights you wouldn't get in any other way.

In contrast, **explicit modeling** is carried out in third position, or the meta position. It's a dissociated and deductive process of working out the specific structure of the role model's subjective experience.

Try this at Home - Simple Modeling Process

1. Find someone that's able to do a simple activity you would like to do.
2. Watch them do it successfully, paying attention to their posture, breathing, gestures, and facial expression.
3. Keep watching until the role model is unsuccessful, and note what is different in their physiology.
4. Have the role model do the task successfully three more times, until you're sure of how to do it.
5. Make an attempt at the skill by generating the same physiology.
6. Keep attempting until you're successful three times.

Simple and Complex Modeling

The process by which the modeling is carried out will depend to a large degree upon what is being modeled. If you want to do something simple, like catching a ball, it may be possible to model it quickly, simply by watching and matching. However, more complex tasks, like public speaking or making sales, require a different approach.

When you're learning how to model it's a good idea to start with simple behaviors. In simple modeling, all you need to pay attention to are the strategies, physiology, and the internal state. After you've mastered this technique, you'll be ready to take on complex modeling, which includes Meta Programs, internal representations, language patterns, and beliefs and values.

The Full Modeling Process

To do a complete modeling process, you're going to need to do every type of modeling. I usually start by deciding whether to model a specific person or a specific skill. If I'm modeling a skill, I'll identify two or three people that are able to do it well. If I choose to model a person, I'll pick a couple of contexts or skills the individual has that I want to model.

The second phase consists of implicit modeling, where you "step in" to the person and feel what its like to be them while they're demonstrating their skill or expertise. This can be done through deep trance identification, or by taking second position.

The third phase is the subtraction phase, or explicit modeling. In this step you take everything you've learned about the model and decide which pieces are necessary in order for the model to work effectively. This is done by subtracting steps, deleting anything that doesn't affect your results. This is critical to ensuring you don't become the model, rather than modeling their skill. This phase is primarily carried out in the meta position, but it also utilizes first position.

The final modeling phase is to use the model. You can either try it on for yourself, or you can teach it to someone else. Of course, if you're modeling Tiger Woods' golf swing, you'll probably need some competency in golf in order to replicate the model. Before using a model successfully, skills may need to be acquired through other means.

For example, if you model the ability to tell great jokes, in order to successfully use the model you've got to know a few jokes.

INDIRECT MODELING

It won't always be practical, or even possible, to spend lots of time with your chosen role model. If they are alive and you're able to speak to them, you can ask lots of questions to understand their beliefs, values, state, Meta Programs, strategies, sub-modalities, and sense of identity. If you meet in person you can observe their physiology, which can be very helpful. But, Indirect Modeling is useful when the model is unavailable but there is information available about how your role model thought, felt, behaved and acted.

The first thing you will always do when modeling is determine exactly what it is you intend to model. Then, find a few individuals that have the skills you desire. Begin by reading biographies and autobiographies of each person, in an effort to determine their strategies, values, and beliefs. Pay specific attention to the commonalities between the strategies to develop the most successful method.

The final step is to teach your conscious and unconscious minds how to operate in a similar way to the thought patterns of the great people you have modeled. The concept is to adapt the strategies to your own personal style to help you achieve your goals.

Try this at Home

1. Specify who and what you are attempting to model
2. Induce a deep trance
3. "Float" into the person you want to model
4. Enter a particular context in which they use the behaviors they are modeling, paying attention to both verbal and nonverbal communication and emotional states
5. Go through several examples over a period of time to strengthen the identification
6. Set an anchor for when to use the model
7. Emerge from trance, and fire off the anchor to test

DEEP TRANCE IDENTIFICATION

Deep trance identification is a process by which a deep state of hypnosis is induced and used to recollect everything known or seen about a particular person and their model of the world. It's a great way to model an individual, because you're able to experience the inner world of the person being modeled. It feels like walking around in someone else's personality, and it can be used to create more compassion and understanding for the model.

Deep trance identification is a fairly simple process, and it's applicable to a variety of situations. Whether you want to pick up a skill or ability from another individual, or if you're looking to experience the world through your spouse's eyes, try this out. I've used it to expand my personality to include more choices of behavior and emotion. I like to think about it like shape shifting. It's all about living from another perspective for a short amount of time. I once did an identification process with my cat. It was very illuminating, and a lot of fun, to be her for a while!

Modeling Worksheet

Who is being modeled? _____

Observations from 3rd Position (Simple Modeling)

Model's nonverbal and verbal communication
Posture _____
Gestures _____
Facial expressions _____
Breathing _____
Word choices _____
Meta Programs _____
Tone of Voice _____

In what environment is the model performing? _____
What behaviors are the model using? _____
What behaviors are intentionally left out? _____
Is the behavior replicated perfectly each time? _____

Experience from 1st Position (Deep Trance Identification)

What emotional state is the model in when performing? _____
What thoughts and internal representations are present? _____
What is the mental strategy being used? _____
What motivates the model to perform? _____
Why do they do this behavior? _____
What is their sense of self/identity? _____
For whom do they do this? _____
Unconscious strategies _____

Complex Modeling, Dissociated (Asking the Model Directly)

What language patterns are they using? _____
What patterns can you find? _____
What emotional state are you in? _____
What are you thinking when ___? _____
What's your strategy? _____
What motivates you? _____
Why do you do this behavior? _____
Who are you that allows you to be successful? _____
For whom do you do this? _____

Chapter 30:
Success Skills

What does success mean to you? Is it a matter of making a certain amount of money, having healthy relationships, developing yourself, having physical fitness, or doing work you love? Take a moment to consider where you could be more successful in your life. Then, play with the processes and concepts that follow. There are several ways NLP can help you become more successful in any area of your life, by helping you achieve peak states, set and achieve goals, manage time effectively, and handle stress.

Peak States

A **peak state** in NLP refers to a state when an individual is performing or feeling at their best. Nearly every individual I have ever encountered has had a peak state experience. A peak state is not necessarily a high energy state, like one you'd have while sky diving. I find the most useful peak states are more grounded, as if everything feels completely natural. Think of it as a state of peak competency.

Peak states are crucial to success in any area of life. There are peak states for communicating, loving, performing, making sales, even for reaching enlightenment. While creating a peak state is fairly simple and straight forward, choosing the appropriate state is critical to your success. So, if you're going to use a role model be sure to choose well. An alternative is to self model by reliving a prior peak state experience in the same context.

Try this at Home- Access a Peak State

1. Straighten your spine, and keep your head and eyes level.
2. Take a few deep breaths into your abdomen, pushing your stomach out as you inhale. Relax the muscles in your spine and limbs.
3. Imagine doing your work from this state, and how much easier it seems.
4. Expand into peripheral vision, by becoming aware of everything beside and behind you.
5. Imagine doing your work again, until it seems very natural.

THE PHYSIOLOGY OF A PEAK STATE

To refresh, physiology refers to the body's physical state at a given time, including: posture, alignment of the spine and head, muscle tension, breathing rate and depth, position of the limbs, facial expression, the direction and focus of the eyes, and gestures and movements. Utilizing peak state physiology can boost your confidence and get you ready to perform.

Peak state physiology can vary from state to state, even person to person. Usually, though, peak states are characterized by an erect spine, deep breathing, relaxed muscles, and a level gaze. You can witness this physiology any time an athlete is "in the zone" or when a performer is giving a great performance.

Whether you make sales calls for a living or you race cars, embodying peak state physiology can improve your success.

GENERATING YOUR OWN PEAK STATE

When it comes to developing a peak state, not only can you experience someone else's, you can create your own. If you take yourself to a time when you were in a peak state, you can anchor that state to use at a later time. Essentially, it's like self modeling.

To model your own peak state, take a moment and remember a time when you really excelled at something. Look at the experience dissociated, noticing your breathing, heart rate, posture, and facial expressions. Associate into the experience, paying attention to how you feel, what you believe, and what's important to you. As you begin to recreate the feelings you had at that time, set a physical anchor. Remember the physiology of this state so that you can practice it often.

GOAL SETTING AND REALIZATION

In Part 2 of this book you learned how to set well formed outcomes. You know that outcomes that are stated in the positive, self initiated and maintained, ecological, represented in visual, auditory, and kinesthetic experiences, and context specific are more likely to be realized. But, did you know that you can place your outcomes on your timeline in order to set everything in motion at a specified time?

The Keys to Success

- Determine what you want
- Create a representation for how to know when you've achieved success
- Model strategies, values, and beliefs for attaining what you desire
- Attach good feelings to doing what it takes to succeed
- Orient your timeline for optimal performance
- Place your goal on your future timeline

The secret to achieving your goals is fairly simple. First, you need to set your outcome. Then you need to be able to imagine it and attach good feelings to doing it. Lastly, you want to place it in your future. Of course, you'll also need to know how to get what you want and how to know when you've become successful, which you can determine using modeling skills.

Once you know what you want, you've got to experience how it feels to have it. You've no doubt heard the expression, "Fake it till you make it." There is a lot of power in that attitude. When you act as if you already have what you want, you engage the unconscious mind to actively recognize it when it appears. Remember that in order to experience feelings, you need to associate into the actual situation. And, by imagining you have what you want, you will be able to feel as if you had it. Ultimately, you want to be able to see an image of your desire, while feeling as if you have it.

You may, at this point, also want to consider how you were able to achieve your desired outcome. By associating into your future and looking back towards the past (your actual present situation), you gain insight into how you came to be where you are. You may discover steps you could take, or people you know that will help you get there. And if you jot all this information down, you'll have a recipe for success. Pay attention to how you motivated yourself, what was difficult, what was easy, and how you overcame challenges to achieve success. Keep in mind, though, that in order for this to work you've got to stay associated into your future.

The final stage in setting your desires in motion is to let them go. Imagine dropping the image of what you want into your future timeline. Release your hold on it, and watch it set in motion of its own accord. Relax, and let it happen. You could specify where it lands, or just let it go where it wants. Either way, watch what takes place to ensure you achieve success. Imagine seeing your success come about on your future timeline. It's so exciting!

Of course, any time you reorient in time to do a process, make sure you reorient into the present before you finish. It will help you to stay present, grounded, and clear.

Meta Programs for Success

In the previous section of this book you learned about Meta Programs in relation to presentation skills. Now let's look at more distinctions that can directly affect your success in specific contexts.

Handling Stress Effectively

One of the most important elements in achieving success is handling stress in an appropriate way. **Feeling** individuals react emotionally to stress, experiencing it very intensely and falling to pieces at the drop of a hat. They are not particularly suited to high stress situations. **Thinking** individuals detach during times of stress, acting in a calm and rational way. They do well under pressure. People with a **Choice** pattern fall somewhere in the middle. They are both compassionate towards others that are stressed, and they can detach from their own stressors in order to get things done.

Personally, I find that Choice is the most useful pattern for the majority of people. However, you want to react in the best way for your particular circumstances. If you work as an Air Traffic Controller, you'd better have a Thinking response to stress. If you are an artist, a Feeling response may be necessary to create.

The best way to change your reaction to stress is to model someone that has the response you desire. Watch them in stressful situations, paying attention to nonverbal communication and verbal communication. Then, try it out in the real world in a stressful situation. Evaluate how you did, then adjust and test it again until you've got it just right.

Motivation Level

The extent to which you're successful can be influenced by your motivation level. Some individuals are highly proactive, actively seeking out situations in which they can succeed. Others prefer to wait for opportunities to come their way, assessing each opportunity to determine the best fit. Now, at first glance, a proactive person seems more likely to be successful. However, both can be equally successful when their strategy adequately fits the situation.

If you're looking to form an intimate relationship, being highly reactive can be detrimental, because if you don't get off the couch you're not likely to meet someone special. On the other hand, if you want to invest millions in a new technology, studying the consequences, analyzing data, and adopting a skeptical approach might be a very appropriate strategy.

The most successful individuals are able to motivate themselves in way that matches the situation. There are times to jump in without thinking too much, and there are times to sit back and consider all sides of a decision. Consider which side you usually take, and expand your choices to include a larger range of behaviors. This is what success is all about.

Rule Structure

Another distinction that directly affects both work and relationship contexts is how we make rules for ourselves and others. A rule is generally based on an individual's beliefs and values, and because of that they can easily change over time or by making an intentional shift.

Someone with a **My/My** rule structure has rules for themselves, and they apply those rules to others. They will often give advice based on their own model of the world, because they believe that people are generally similar. This can come in handy if you're an expert in a field, but it's a good pattern to avoid if you're not.

An individual with a **My/Your** rule structure believes that people are generally different, and so they allow others to have their own rules. They tend to be compassionate, but others may see this as wishy-washy, because they don't take a stand on most issues. It's too easy for them to see all sides of an argument. That makes this a pattern best suited to parenting, because it allows children to develop their own identity without being overly programmed by their role models. This is also a trait I look for in my NLP students, because a good practitioner doesn't give advice, they skillfully lead their clients to find their own answers. I believe Milton Erickson had this pattern.

If you have ever lived with someone that slammed doors in the middle of the night or always ate the last bite of a shared dish, you've encountered the **My/No** pattern. These individuals have rules for themselves, and they aren't at all concerned with others. They come across as selfish, but they really just don't notice that they are affecting others, because they themselves aren't affected. They just do what they need to do. These people are particularly suited to completing tasks that don't involve people, which is not easy to find. This pattern can be extremely difficult within relationships, unless both individuals have it.

Individuals with a **No/My** structure are very adept at leading others, but they're usually unsuccessful in making decisions for themselves. They tend to be associated in their own lives, with an inability to dissociate long enough to get clarity about their own situation. However, if you teach a person with this pattern how to dissociate, they can often get their answers very quickly. This pattern is valued in the military and in middle management, where individuals have to enforce the rules but don't necessarily have a say in developing them.

To shift your particular rule structure, you may need to shift your beliefs about whether people are generally the same or different. You may need to learn how to dissociate in order to get clarity, or associate into another person's model of the world. I personally find the ability to shift from one pattern to another is the most useful. There are times to take a stand and lead others, and there are times to manage your own life. Consider what would be best for you right now with your particular goals and ambitions.

Convincing Strategies

I've had the opportunity to work with some excellent sales professionals, and I've learned how important it is to be able convince others. And when I think about it, I realize that teachers, lecturers, politicians, and parents all have to do some convincing. If you want to be able to get your point across to another individual, you need to know how they get convinced.

There are two main aspects to becoming convinced: how you receive information and how you treat that information. People receive information by **Seeing, Hearing, Reading,** or **Doing**. A vast majority of individuals prefer to see something, either in writing or as an image, with needing to hear something coming in second. So, when presenting your ideas to others, make sure you provide visual, auditory, and kinesthetic evidence of your claims. You're far more likely to persuade the listener when you provide a variety of evidence.

People also have a convincer mode. Some need a particular **Number of Examples** of a specific type of evidence. I have a friend that needs to hear something three times before he's convinced that it's true. So, if he wants to change a limiting belief, all I need to do is to tell him the new belief three times. It works every time! Some individuals have an **Automatic** convincer strategy, which is like giving someone the benefit of the doubt. This is a double edged sword, because while it's easy to convince them of something, if they already have a particular belief it's difficult to change their mind. People with a **Period of Time** convincer are fairly easy to work with. All they need is a certain amount of time with someone or something to be sure how they feel about it. **Consistent** convincers are never truly convinced. These individuals need to re-evaluate on a constant basis. These people make difficult customers, because they're never really sold on a brand. They will need to test each individual product or service each time they use it.

I've found that knowing a customer's convincer mode is extremely helpful. But it also applies within relationships. You may find yourself having to convince your teenager to avoid harmful influences. Or, you may want to convince your spouse to remodel the kitchen. The possibilities are numerous.

To determine someone's convincer, ask them, "How often do you have to demonstrate ____ before you're convinced?" From their answer, you'll be able to tell into which category they fit. Then, use that information to convince them. For example, when I asked a client of mine how often he needed to respond differently to his father before he'd be sure he had made a permanent change, he said, "I suppose I'd be sure after a month of healthy interaction." So, I took him through a progression process. He experienced a variety of healthy interactions with his father over the next month, and by the time it had been a month he was feeling much more confident in his ability to make the change.

In a sales setting, you may want to ask a potential customer how often they need to see or hear about a new product before they're willing to buy it. If the person says, "If it's new I want it," show them a new product, and tell them to buy it. That's all it will take! However, if they respond with, "I heard about this new car a few times before I was willing to take a test drive," the person probably just needs to hear a few positive benefits before they're convinced to buy. Potentially they will need to test drive it more than once or see it in a few different colors, particularly if they also need to see or do in order to be convinced.

SUMMARY

Now that you know a variety of ways to increase your success in your life and work, I encourage you to go out and try out these techniques and patterns. Pick one thing you wish to improve, and use a particular strategy I've presented in a variety of situations until your ability to use it generalizes to a variety of situations. Keep in mind that the definition of success is choice and flexibility. If you are able to adjust your emotions, beliefs, and behaviors from context to context, you'll always have the advantage.

The most obvious way to increase choice and flexibility is through modeling. Modeling expands your skill set by utilizing the three perceptual positions, giving you a variety of perspectives for any situation. By using more than one role model for a specific skill, you also gain more options for how you personally wish to employ that skill. Modeling adds choices by opening you to new feelings and emotions as well.

When modeling, you need to gather information. This can be done by asking the appropriate and relevant questions, or through deep trance identification. My preference is to do both to verify the integrity of your information. The main pieces of information you want to gather is:

- Beliefs
- Values
- Internal Representations & Sub-modalities
- Strategies

- Physiology & Tonality
- The goal of the behavior
- Sensory evidence in regards to the goal
- The choices being made and the behaviors used to support them
- The response to not achieving the goal
- How the model fits into each logical level.

Other ways to increase your success by expanding your choices is through modeling or generating peak states, creating an appropriate stress response, becoming more proactive in certain areas of life, and by creating a flexible rule structure. Remember, though, there is no substitute for setting achievable outcomes and building motivation to carry out the behaviors necessary for success.

STUDY QUESTIONS

1. What are the pros and cons to deep trance identification and indirect modeling?
2. What elements of a person's experience should be left out of a model?
3. On which logical level does most modeling occur?
4. How do you create a peak state?

Conclusion

After reading this book, I hope that you've found some simple, practical tips for improving your life and work. You've probably generated new behaviors, gained new capabilities, and shifted some beliefs. You may have even expanded your identity. What's the big reason for making these changes for you? For me, NLP is about becoming more conscious.

I've traveled the world doing this work, and everywhere I go I meet people living on auto-pilot. They take life as it comes, sometimes resisting experiences with the rigidity of stubbornness. Others do a form of jiu-jitsu, bending and using negative experiences to increase their happiness and success. To me, truly embracing NLP is an act of conscious creation. What would happen if you lived every day on purpose? If you could consciously create your thoughts, shift your attitudes, and act in accord with resourceful beliefs, how successful would you be?

If you could honestly look beyond what is to what could be and feel inspired to create it, how would your life be different? It is my sincere desire that every reader be inspired to take the wisdom embodied in this model of the world and spread it to at least one other person in their life. If everyone on this planet truly understood that life is simply a series of choices, what would we do differently? I tend to believe we'd make better decisions about how we treat other and our Earth. So let's do it... now.

GLOSSARY OF TERMS

4-Tuple - A method used to notate the structure of an experience; based on the concept that any experience must be composed of some combination of the four primary representational systems (Auditory, Visual, Kinesthetic, and Olfactory/Gustatory).

Accessing cues - Physiological behaviors that can both trigger and indicate the representational system being used in a person's thoughts; includes eye movements, voice tone, tempo, body posture, gestures, and breathing patterns.

Anchoring - The process of associating an internal response with an external trigger (similar to classical conditioning) so that the emotional and behavioral response may be re-accessed.

As If frame - Derived from the work of Milton Erickson; involves taking an individual into the future to a point in which their problem is solved in order to determine how it was done; used to bypass resistance to finding one's own answers.

Association - Seeing, hearing and feeling the present moment; reliving a memory; used for accessing emotional states or adding resources to a particular memory or future experience.

Auditory - Relating to the sense of hearing.

Auditory internal - Self talk; internal dialogue.

Backtracking - A verbal and non-verbal review of the last portion of a person's communication.

Behavior - Physical actions and reactions through which we interact with the people and environment around us, including posture, gestures, facial expressions, and other deliberate actions and body movements.

BMIR - Behavioral manifestation of an internal response; external evidence of an emotion that can be calibrated.

Calibration - The process of noticing an individual's nonverbal communication; used to determine the link between a person's internal state and external behavior; often appears as "mind reading" to outside observers.

Cause and effect - A belief with the structure x=y.

Chunking - The process of grouping experience; chunking down gets to a more specific and concrete level of information; chunking up generates a more abstract or exaggerated level of information.

Complex equivalence - A belief with the structure x means y; the meaning attributed to an event or experience.

Congruence - When all of an individual's internal beliefs, strategies, and behaviors (or parts) are fully in agreement and aligned with securing a specific desired outcome.

Context - The framework surrounding an event that affects how that particular experience is interpreted by the individual; where, when, and with whom an event occurs.

Conversational hypnosis - Bypassing the critical factor and generating selective attention in the waking state through complex language patterns and rapport; the use of the Milton Model and Sleight of Mouth patterns to effect change and influence on an individual while in an uptime trance.

Criteria - The values or rules a person uses to make decisions; secondary gain of a problem; can be determined by chunking up from the behavioral level.

Deep structure - The conscious and unconscious maps of reality that individuals use to organize and guide their behavior; an individual's representations of their beliefs and experiences.

Deep trance identification - The process of inducing a deep state of hypnosis for the purposes of modeling an individual; used to recollect everything an individual has ever known or seen of a role model by pretending to be that individual in order to experience and identify with their world completely.

Deletion - The process of leaving relevant information out of a communication; deleted information is gathered with the Meta Model by asking *how, who,* and *what*; information is purposely deleted in the Milton Model to create a deeper trance state in a subject.

Desired state - What an individual or group wants to create; the feelings, thoughts, behaviors, beliefs, and values that support what is desired.

Dissociation – The meta perceptual position; observing self in an event or memory for the purposes of disconnecting feelings or gaining learning; three place dissociation, or the state created by observing the observer, is used for processing traumatic memories.

Distortion - The act of changing the meaning of a communication; in the Meta Model, these limiting beliefs are challenged by asking how the meaning was created.

Embedded Command - A hypnotic suggestion embedded within a larger sentence structure that is marked out by varying volume, tonality, or using a specific gesture.

Future pacing - The process of mentally taking oneself through a variety imagined future contexts in which a change must occur in order to ensure that the desired behavioral change will occur naturally and automatically, without negative ramifications.

Generalization - The process by which components of a person's model of the world become detached from their original experience and come to represent the entire category of which the experience is merely a sample.

Gestalt - A cluster of memories in which there is a common emotional experience; accessed through an affect bridge when conducting regression therapy.

Hypnosis - The bypass of the critical factor and creation of selective attention for the purposes of giving suggestions, influencing behavior, or retrieving information.

Incongruence – The state of having conflicting values and/or beliefs; indecision; having parts in conflict; bi-lateral incongruence is a difference in the appearance between the left and right sides of the body, which indicates an inner conflict.

Kinesthetic - Relating to tactile, visceral, and emotional feelings and sensations.

Leading - The act of using an existing rapport with an individual to take them into a different state; done by changing verbal and nonverbal communication to match the desired state.

Logical Levels - A model, originating from the work of Gregory Bateson, for defining the levels of human experience and how those levels influence each other; used in information gathering and modeling; consists of environment, behaviors, capabilities, beliefs, identity, and spirituality.

Matching - The act of copying a person's nonverbal communication for the purpose of building rapport.

Meta Model - Identifies categories of language patterns that can be problematic or ambiguous; used to gather specific information and generate clear communication; the reverse of the Milton Model.

Meta Program - A process by which an individual sorts through multiple generalizations simultaneously; Meta Programs control how and when a person will utilize a strategy in a given context; often used in personality profiling.

Metaphors - Stories, parables and analogies commonly used to instruct or make changes in the unconscious mind; used to bypass conscious resistance to change.

Milton Model - A set of language patterns derived from the work of Milton Erickson by Bandler and Grinder; how to use indirect suggestion in conversational hypnosis to influence behavior and effect change; the reverse of the Meta Model with a few added patterns.

Mirroring - The act of creating a mirror image of a person's body movements and gestures for the purpose of building rapport.

Modal operators - Verbs that modify how an action is done, as in *I have to get up* or *I could get up*; operators of possibility include can, could, might, want to, may; operators of necessity include must, have to, should, need to, will, won't.

Modeling - The act of gathering information from one individual and applying it to another individual for the purpose of transferring skills, abilities, and strategies; implicit modeling is done by copying nonverbal behaviors; explicit modeling is done through observation of the role model.

More-More pattern - The process of using an individual's resistance to influence their behavior in a positive way, as in *the more you resist closing your eyes the more relaxed you feel.*

Nominalizations - Verbs restructured to sound like nouns; nouns that describe a process, as in the word *relationship* describing the act of relating to another.

Neuro-Linguistic Programming - The study of the structure of subjective experience and what can be calculated from it.

Pacing - A method used to quickly establish rapport by matching certain aspects of behavior to those of the person with whom you are communicating; matching or mirroring behavior.

Parts - A metaphorical way of talking about aspects of the personality and strategies of behavior; used to separate a behavior from the positive intention, or motivating criteria, behind it.

Pattern interrupt - A process used to disconnect a trigger from the operation of a problem strategy; done by shifting a person's attention away from the problem after a trigger is fired off; used to break bad habits, allergies, and emotional addictions.

Peak state - A state in which a person is able to excel in their chosen activity or profession.

Perceptual positions – A process of viewing an event from different points of view; first position is an association to self and is used in NLP to relive or add resources to an experience; second position is an association to other and is used to gather learning about another person's thoughts, feelings, values, and beliefs; third position is the meta position, or the observer, which is used to gather learning from an event by seeing all the sides of an issue.

Phobia - An intense or irrational fear of an object or event.

Placebo effect - the measurable, observable, or experienced change in health or behavior not attributable to a medication or invasive treatment that has been administered; a change that can be attributed to a person's belief or expectation in the treatment or the practitioner.

Predicates - Process words (like verbs, adverbs, and adjectives) that a person selects to describe a subject; used to identify which representational system a person is using to process information; can be sensory or non-sensory.

Present state - An individual's current behaviors, thoughts, feelings, values, and beliefs within a particular context; usually the problem state in therapy.

Presupposition - A meaning, not explicitly stated, that can be derived from an utterance, as in *how many clowns were there* presupposes at least one was in attendance.

Rapport - The presence of trust, harmony, and cooperation in a relationship; generated by pacing an individual's verbal and nonverbal communication.

Representational systems - The senses; seeing, hearing, feeling, smelling and tasting.

Role model – An individual with a desired skill or capability; can be utilized in the first and second perceptual positions for the purpose of modeling.

Root cause – The earliest sensitizing event in a gestalt; regression therapy aims to uncover the root cause in order to gain learning and disconnect negative emotions from that event and from all the subsequent events in the gestalt in order to change a future response to a similar event.

Secondary gain - Where some seemingly negative or problematic behavior actually carries out some positive function at another level; commonly referred to as the intention behind behavior.

Strategies - A set of explicit mental and behavioral steps used to achieve a specific outcome; *how* we do what we do; the T.O.T.E. model identifies the trigger, operation, test, and exit phases of a particular strategy.

Submodalities - The sensory qualities perceived by each of the five senses; visual submodalities include color, shape, movement, brightness, depth, etc.; auditory submodalities include volume, pitch, tempo, etc.; kinesthetic submodalities include pressure, temperature, texture, location, etc.

Surface Structure - A verbal utterance.

Systematic desensitization - a form of treatment in which a dissociated trance subject is led to replace an unpleasant feeling with a resource a little bit at a time, ensuring the change is made comfortably and completely; a way to reduce fear in a phobic subject by having them imagine getting closer to the feared object while maintaining calm.

Timeline - The structure of how an individual organizes experiences; an in-time timeline runs front to back and is associated; a through-time timeline runs left to right and is dissociated; used as a regression tool and for increasing organizational skills.

Universal quantifiers - Words that indicate a generalization of an experience; all, every, never, always, none, each; often challenged using the Meta Model.

Utilization – The act of using any event or response to further one's intent; the use of a client's resistance to move them forward with their goals, as in the more-more pattern; acting as if whatever occurs was intended and useful.

Visual - Relating to the sense of sight.

Well-Formed Outcomes – Desired states that fit the following criteria: stated in the positive, initiated and maintained by self, context specific, represented in sensory experience, preserves the positive byproducts of the present state, and ecological.

References

Andreas, Steve and Connirae Andreas. *Change Your Mind and Keep the Change*. Moab, Utah: Real People Press, 1987.

Bandler, Richard and John Grinder. *Patterns of the Hypnotic Techniques of Milton H. Erickson, M.D. Volume 1*. Capitola, CA: Meta Publications, 1975.

Bandler, Richard and John Grinder. *Patterns of the Hypnotic Techniques of Milton H. Erickson, M.D. Volume 2*. Capitola, CA: Meta Publications, 1977.

Bandler, Richard and John LaValle. *Persuasion Engineering*. Capitola, CA: Meta Publications, 1996.

Bandler, Richard. Using Your Brain for a Change. Moab, Utah: Real People Press, 1985.

Begley, Sharon. *Train Your Mind, Change Your Brain*. New York: Ballantine Books, 2007.

Charvet, Shelle Rose. *Words that Change Minds*. Dubuque, IA: Kendall/Hunt Publishing Company, 1995.

Dilts, Robert. *Sleight of Mouth*. Capitola, California: Meta Publications, 2006.

Dilts, Robert, Tim Hallbom, and Suzi Smith. *Beliefs: Pathways to Health & Well-being*. Portland, OR: Metamorphous Press, 1990.

Dilts, Robert and Robert Mcdonald. *Tools of the Spirit*. Capitola, CA: Meta Publications, 1997.

Dilts, Robert, John Grinder, Richard Bandler, and Judith Delozier. *Neuro-Linguistic Programming, Volume 1: The Study of the Structure of Subjective Experience*. Capitola, CA: Meta Publications, 1980.

Goleman, Daniel. *Emotional Intelligence: Why it can Matter More than IQ*. New York: Bantam, 1995.

Grinder, John and Richard Bandler. *Trance-Formations*. Moab, Utah: Real People Press, 1981.

Grinder, John, and Richard Bandler. *The Patterns and Techniques of Dr. Milton H. Erickson, M.D., Volume I*. Portland, OR: Metamorphous Press, 1975.

Grinder, John, Judith Delozier, and Richard Bandler. *The Patterns and Techniques of Dr. Milton H. Erickson, M.D., Volume II*. Portland, OR: Metamorphous Press, 1975.

O'Connor, Joseph and John Seymour. *Introducing NLP: Psychological Skills for Understanding and Influencing People*. Hammersmith, London: Thorsons, 1995.

Pert, Candace B. *Molecules of Emotion: The Science Behind Mind-Body Medicine*. New York: Simon & Schuster, 1997.

BLOGS

www.usinghumor.com
Brantley, Dan. *Hearing Yourself.*

www.Hypnosis 101.com
Livingston, Keith. *Dr. Phil, Her Butt, and Ambiguity.*

www.MayoClinic.com
Phobias. January 10, 2009.

www.renewal.ca
Ellerton, Roger. *The Milton Model.*

www.nlm.nih.gov/medlineplus
Asthma.

Resources

I hope you have enjoyed reading this text. Because NLP has so many applications for improving your life and work, I have developed several seminars and training programs to take what you've learned here and incorporate it into your every day life. Some seminars focus on corporate communications, while others target improving intimate relationships. Certification as an NLP Practitioner or Master Practitioner is also available.

Available Programs
The Building Blocks of Success
The Happiness Quest
How to Play Well With Others
Hypnotherapy Certification
Past Life Regression Certification
NLP Practitioner Certification
NLP Master Practitioner Certification

Websites
www.janisericson.com
The author's blog and training schedule also has information on booking private sessions and corporate seminars. Find all the author's products and courses here.

www.hybridnlp.com

A great resource for learning NLP at home, this company provides certification through a hybrid of distance learning and live training. There is also a recommended reading list and bookstore.

www.lightworkseminars.com

Lightwork Seminars, Intl is a leader in providing live training in NLP, Hypnosis, Reiki, and ThetaHealing, with courses around the globe. This is also a great resource for books, hypnosis CDs and training DVDs. 415-491-1122